TRILBY JAMES

Trilby James read Drama at Bristol University before completing the three-year acting course at RADA. She graduated in 1990 and over the years has worked extensively as an actor in theatre and television. In 2000 she also began working as a freelance director and teacher at several leading drama schools including ALRA, Arts Educational Schools, Royal Central School of Speech and Drama, East 15, Mountview Academy of Theatre Arts, Manchester Metropolitan University and the Royal Academy of Dramatic Art where she is now an Associate Teacher. She continues to work across courses, directing third-year performances as well as teaching first and second-year students, MA students and running workshops for shorter programmes. She is a script reader and dramaturg for Kali Theatre Company and has directed several play-readings for their 'Talkback' seasons.

THE GOOD AUDITION GUIDES

AUDITION SONGS
edited by Paul Harvard

CONTEMPORARY DUOLOGUES
edited by Trilby James

CLASSICAL MONOLOGUES
edited by Marina Caldarone

CONTEMPORARY MONOLOGUES
edited by Trilby James

CONTEMPORARY MONOLOGUES FOR TEENAGERS
edited by Trilby James

SHAKESPEARE MONOLOGUES
edited by Luke Dixon

SHAKESPEARE MONOLOGUES FOR YOUNG PEOPLE
edited by Luke Dixon

The Good Audition Guides

CONTEMPORARY MONOLOGUES FOR TEENAGERS: MALE

edited and introduced by

TRILBY JAMES

NHB

NICK HERN BOOKS
London
www.nickhernbooks.co.uk

A NICK HERN BOOK

The Good Audition Guides:
Contemporary Monologues for Teenagers: Male
first published in Great Britain in 2019
by Nick Hern Books Limited
The Glasshouse, 49a Goldhawk Road, London W12 8QP

Designed and typeset by Nick Hern Books, London
Printed and bound by CPI Books (UK) Ltd

A CIP catalogue record for this book
is available from the British Library

ISBN 978 1 84842 607 8

Contents

Introduction

☞ WHAT THIS BOOK OFFERS

Whether you are taking theatre studies at school level, auditioning for drama school or simply enjoying an after-school drama group, a contemporary monologue that has been specifically written for your own age group, and reflects the concerns of young people, will be a great starting point. The forty monologues in this volume are from plays that have been written post-2000. The characters range in age from fourteen to nineteen. There is a wide variety of character types and styles of writing from which to choose. They are all drawn from the extensive list of new plays published by Nick Hern Books.

A Warning:

Some of the plays are specifically about the abuse of teenage girls and may not be suitable for readers under sixteen. In the theatre these parts would have been played by young adult actors, so in this volume they come with the following trigger warning: 'This play deals with adult themes. It has content and language that some readers might find disturbing or offensive.'

☞ CHOOSING YOUR MONOLOGUE

I have often likened finding the perfect monologue to finding the perfect pair of jeans. It is rarely a case of 'one size fits all'. You might have to try on several pairs, in different shops, before you find the cut that works for you, but once you have, you will feel confident in the knowledge that you are looking and feeling your best. So it is with audition speeches. You need to find pieces that suit you, that you cannot wait to get in to and that will feel even better with wear.

If you are auditioning for a youth theatre:

- You will be judged on your potential and your willingness to be open, honest and free. Nobody is looking for a polished or over-rehearsed performance. It is best therefore to choose pieces that allow you to express yourself and for a panel to see something of who you really are.
- Choose something close to you in age and type. Something to which you can relate. Something that inspires you, from a play that speaks to you.

If you are auditioning for drama school:

- And have also been asked to prepare a classical speech, choose a contemporary monologue that will provide contrast. For example, you may have a Shakespearean monologue that is pensive or tragic, so opt for something comic. Similarly, if your classical speech is light in tone, choose a companion piece that shows off a more serious side.

If you are already at drama school:

- And you are looking to extend your range, you will want to choose a monologue that stretches you. Perhaps you are studying a particular accent or type of character quite different from yourself.
- Or you are looking for showcase material, think about how you wish to present yourself. Consider whether you are right for the part you have chosen and whether, if you had a chance to be in a production of the play, you could be easily cast in the role.

If you are auditioning for a specific role in a professional production (and have been asked to prepare an additional piece that is not from the play for which you are being seen):

- Choose something close to the part for which you are auditioning.
- Consider the language of the piece and whether you are after something heightened and obviously theatrical, or whether you require something more intimate and realistic.

If you are looking to extend your showreel:

- It may sound obvious, but think about what sort of speeches would be best suited to the varying demands of radio, film or television.

☞ PREPARING YOUR MONOLOGUE

- Learn your speeches well in advance of the actual audition. Should you forget your lines, the panel will be able to tell whether it is out of nervousness or insufficient preparation.
- Read the whole play. You may be asked questions about it or be required to improvise around it.
- Undertake all necessary research. Make a study of the historical, social and political world of the play. Be sure to understand the meaning of unfamiliar words and references.
- Accents: By and large it is best to avoid accents unless you are really good at them or want an opportunity to practise them. If a character's accent is not native to you, you may like to try playing it in your own accent. However, watch out for speeches that have been written with a strong dialect or idiom and where the essential rhythm of the piece needs to be maintained.
- Remain flexible in the way you perform/stage your monologue. Be prepared to be redirected in an audition.
- Talking to the audience: If your character is talking to the audience, make a decision about who the audience are to you. Are they your friend and your confidante? Are they more like an analyst with whom you feel safe to reveal your innermost thoughts? Are they a sort of sounding board? Are they judging you? Do you need to explain yourself or to convince them in some way? It is still advisable not to look at the actual panel in this case, but imagine an audience just above their heads and direct your speech there.

- Using props: There are no hard-and-fast rules about the use of stage properties at an audition. However, common sense suggests that, if you can easily carry an object in your pocket (e.g. a letter, a ring, a handkerchief, etc.), by all means bring this to an audition. If the object to which you refer is large, imagine it is there, or, if necessary, mime using it. Some might even argue that miming props is simpler, and in certain cases much more practical. In any event, you need not worry about being 'marked down' by your decision either to use real objects or to mime using them. What is important is that they do not become burdensome and get in the way of your acting.
- What to wear: Again there are no set rules about this, but I would suggest that to help you make a connection to your character you try to dress like them. If the character is formal or from another time in history, trousers and a shirt and tie as opposed to jeans and a T-shirt will make a huge difference. Similarly there is a very different feel when you wear hard shoes as opposed to trainers. When I was at drama school, our acting teacher used to refer to 'costume' as 'garments', and we would be encouraged to rehearse in appropriate clothing. In this way we thought of costume not as a thing that got added at the end, but as something that was as personal to us as our own everyday wardrobe.
- Try not to get stuck in a mode of delivery. It is useful to consider that, unless a character is making a political or after-dinner speech, chances are they have no idea they are going to speak for such a long time. They may make a statement, perhaps as a response to a specific question; then having made that statement they might need to qualify it. They might then be reminded of something else they wish to add and so on. In this way, a monologue can be regarded as a series of interrelated thoughts. Communicating a character's thought processes is fundamental to any acting technique. In the case of an audition, it takes the pressure off having to deliver a load of text. It allows you to stay fresh, to be in the moment and to make spontaneous choices. Before you start, all you need

worry about is the trigger – the reason for saying what you do. Then have the courage to take it thought by thought and allow yourself to be surprised. In this way the monologue should feel slightly different every time.

- It is vital that you use your imagination to envisage all that the character sees and describes. If you are still seeing the page on which the speech is written, you know you are doing something wrong. Provide images for yourself so that in your mind's eye you quite literally lift the speech from the page.
- Timing/editing: Most speeches at audition should last no longer than two minutes. Some of the monologues in this volume are slightly longer, some shorter. Some I have cut, and some I have edited from dialogue with another character, and some have been augmented by joining two or more passages which appear separately in the original text. I have inserted this empty bracket symbol [...] to show where a cut has been made. Once you have read the whole play, you may have ideas of your own about what and what not to include.

☞ THE AUDITION

You will find there are many useful books on the market that make a complete study of this subject, from what to wear to how to enter and exit a room. These are some of the basics:

- Manage your nerves. Try to put the increased adrenaline you are experiencing to good use. Approach the audition with a positive sense of excitement, something to which you have been looking forward as opposed to something you have been dreading. Nervous energy, if correctly channelled, can help at an audition. Conversely you should avoid being under-energised. If you are someone who reacts lethargically to increased stress, you may need to do a good warm-up before you arrive.
- Take ownership of the situation. Before you begin, take a moment to imagine the space you are in as the location of

the monologue. The best auditions are those in which the actor successfully transports the panel from 'Studio One' (or whatever the room you are auditioning in is called) to an urban street, a clearing in the woods, a grand room in a stately home, etc. Take time to think about where you will place the other character/s in the scene and, before you speak, allow yourself a moment to hear what has been said to you or to imagine what has just happened that prompts you to say the things you do. Do not rush the speech. Take your time. In the case of a drama-school audition, remember that you will be paying for this privilege!

- Empower yourself. There is no good reason why the panel should want you to fail. If you are auditioning for a youth group or a drama school, consider that the panel are willing you to do well, even if they are not necessarily giving that impression. If you have been asked to be seen for a specific role, it is because the director is serious about you for the job. It is possible that the panel are equally anxious about the impression they may give you. Remember, you only have control over your part of the audition process. There is no point speculating, worrying about whether they will want you in their group, grant you a place in their school or offer you the part. Just take care of your side of things, and be safe in the knowledge that, whatever happens, you tried your best.

☞ HOW TO USE THIS BOOK

For each of the monologues I have provided a bullet-point list of ten things you need to know about the character. These will include their age and where they come from, a bit about their background and what sort of personality they have. In some instances these facts are already contained within the monologue. Then I have suggested five things to help you perform the monologue. These will include objectives to play and ideas about how to connect to your character. They will also touch on the subjects already covered in this introduction such as using props, talking to the audience, accents and what to wear, etc. You will also need to read the whole play so that you can build a bigger picture. As you become increasingly familiar with your monologue, you will soon develop ideas of your own and may even find yourself in disagreement with my notes. Acting is a very personal thing, and no two actors, like any two people, will think exactly alike. I hope that this book will be a source of inspiration and ultimately get you thinking for yourself.

The Monologues

About a Goth*

Tom Wells

TEN THINGS YOU NEED TO KNOW ABOUT NICK:

- Nick is seventeen.
- He is a goth.
- He is gay.
- He is intelligent and highly (perhaps overly) sensitive.
- He is in love with a boy called Greg.
- He lives with his mum and dad, and sister Lizzie.
- His family are kind, caring, 'normal' and happy.
- Nick likes to pretend that his life has been tragic.
- He loves reading the work of the French Existentialists. (I would suggest reading *The Outsider* by Albert Camus if you haven't already done so.)
- Nick hates to be part of the herd. He loves to think that he is special or different from most people.

FIVE THINGS TO HELP YOU PERFORM THE MONOLOGUE:

- The speech is very funny, but Nick is deadly serious. See if you can find his tragic tone as he tries to persuade us that his life is doomed.
- Nick is talking to the audience (see note on talking to the audience in the introduction). Make a decision about who we might be to him.
- There is a lot of contrast between the ordinary or mundane things in Nick's life and Nick's own romantic or elevated view of himself. Observe, for example, the way he manages to translate a grotty bus stop into something more meaningful by

* Published in the volume *Me, As A Penguin* by Tom Wells

saying 'it smells of piss and *regret*'. Perhaps with your own interest in drama and acting you can relate to his need to make his life appear more fascinating/dramatic than it actually is.

- The speech contains within it several different locations. You will really need to picture all the places that he describes in order for the monologue to take shape. And see if you can imagine all the objects, from the Ikea bed to the graves in the cemetery.
- As well as picturing all that Nick can see, consider what he hears, tastes, smells and touches. There are many things of a sensory nature in the speech. Be aware of all the things he eats and drinks. The more vivid these things are for you, the more effective the monologue will be.

NB This play offers a number of other monologues from which to choose.

Nick

“As beds go it is passable, I suppose. Obviously I would prefer to sleep in a coffin but as my mum has so hilariously pointed out, they don't sell coffins at Ikea.
Yet.

[...]

I check my phone but. Nothing. Greg still hasn't replied to my text. It has been three days and eleven hours now, which seems a bit relaxed even for someone as simple as him. Look in my sent messages. It's there in capital letters:
I HATE MYSELF AND I WANT TO DIE.
I wonder if I've been too subtle again. Probably. I forget not everyone is as emotionally mature and sensitive as me. I decide to have a wank, but even that is doomed. Halfway through, I start worrying about getting stains on my new black duvet cover. My heart isn't in it after that. [...]

Breakfast is depressing as usual. All I want is to read Camus and eat my Coco Pops, but it is so hard to concentrate with Dad's armour clanking and Mum clattering about with her

tankards in the sink. [...] Honestly. It's tragic. Everyone else's parents lie and cheat and have inner turmoil and chuck teapots at each other. I get the world's most cheerful medieval re-enactors. My mum leans over, dangles her fluted sleeve in my chocolatey milk, passes me a postcard. It's got a donkey on the front. Looking jaunty.
'Camping is amazing.'
Three exclamation marks.
'Weather perfect.'
A further two exclamation marks.
'Dropped my phone off a cliff to prove it is shatterproof. It's not. That was my old phone. Brilliant.'
Underlined.
'Bet your missing me.'
'Your' spelt wrong.
'You big gay.'
No comment.
'Greg.'
And a kiss.

Pause.

'Fancy finishing off this mead?'
Mum holds out a bottle.
I give her a long, stern look.
'Wench, I do not.'

The bus isn't due for another ten minutes so I undo one of my badges and self-harm for a bit. I don't draw blood cos my cloak is dry clean only but it helps pass the time. The bus stop smells of piss and regret. It's a very sunny day, the worst kind of weather for a goth, so I lurk in the shadows contemplating the great tragedies of my life. The burden of my intelligence, for example. Loneliness.
I am an only child.
Unless you count Lizzie, my sister [...]

Right on cue, she drives past the bus stop. [...]

'Alright, gorgeous,' she says.
I could vom.
'Need a lift into town?' [...]

I get dropped off at the mini-roundabout. There is a sense of foreboding and quite a big Starbucks. I buy a Mint Frappuccino, the most gothic of the available drinks, and finish it in the cemetery next door. [...] I've got a muffin too but I'm saving it till afterwards. Give me something to live for. Cos looking round me, the graves have never seemed more inviting. In the end, though, it's time. I slurp the last minty dregs and head off for another two hours of misery. ”

Blue Stockings

Jessica Swale

TEN THINGS YOU NEED TO KNOW ABOUT LLOYD:

- The play is set in 1896.
- Lloyd is aged between eighteen to nineteen.
- He comes from a highly privileged background.
- He is studying science at Trinity College, Cambridge.
- Along with the men at Cambridge, who form the vast majority of students, there are a handful of girls at Girton College, who are also studying science. Lloyd is dismissive of them as he strongly believes that a woman's place is in the home.
- Today we might describe Lloyd as a 'misogynist', but then he was simply upholding the values and opinions of the time.
- He is clever and could be on track for a double first.
- He is very much 'one of the lads', and enjoys drinking and joking around.
- He is physically strong and fit and enjoys mountaineering.
- We don't know an awful lot about LLoyd's family background. See if you can use the opportunity to create a backstory for yourself. Think about where he comes from, his family relationships, etc., and why in particular he is so down on the emancipation of women.

FIVE THINGS TO HELP YOU PERFORM THE MONOLOGUE:

- Girton was the first college in Britain to admit female students, and 1896 saw the first intake. However, when women finished their studies they were denied the right to graduate and to receive a degree. Read the whole play and make time to research these facts.

- The scene is set in a haberdasher's shop where the boys from Trinity have bumped into two of the girls from Girton. The girls are buying material for a banner in order to protest for their right to graduate. See if you can imagine what the girls look like so that you have a focus for the monologue.
- Lloyd is as passionate about women not getting degrees as the women who are campaigning for them. Although you probably don't share his views, for the monologue to work it is important that you do not demonise him. See if you can adopt the mindset of the time. He genuinely believes that studying will be bad for women's health. He is also scared of what might happen if women become as powerful as men.
- He uses harsh and caustic language, and even his fellow male students are shocked at his rudeness. I would further suggest that this hatred of women goes beyond the common thinking of the day and has something to do with Lloyd's own personal feelings about women. What causes a man to be a misogynist? Has he had a difficult relationship with his mother or other women in his family? You decide.
- When you get to the list of all the men who have 'made this nation', be aware of what exactly each one of these famous men did and achieved. Research them all. A good tip when your speech includes a list is to create momentum by having a *new* thought with each and everyone of them. In this way you build the list from the top of your head rather than recite it as if you were reading from a pre-written shopping list.

Lloyd

“What would you do with a degree anyway? Run the country? Be an engineer? Develop a cure for smallpox? […] And who are you going to doctor, miss? Me? Him? No? Who? […] Who?! […] No man will be doctored by a woman, […] no man will employ you. No man will take your directions. No man will vote for you. So you're a lost cause. Why fight it? […] (*Explodes suddenly.*) Listen! I was at school at five. At seven I knew Plato. At twelve, hand me a cadaver and I'd tell you the name of every last nerve in it. You think you can compete? You think some tuppenny once-a-week governess is enough, do you? Some tattered notes from your brother? Some village dunce school for girls? You think *that* – that joke of an education – gives you a right to set foot here? At Cambridge? Cambridge, for God's sake! This isn't some country-hole second-rate pauper's college. We're not average men here. We are the future. The leaders. The establishment. We don't sleep, we don't rest, we don't give up and we don't come second. We learn. It's our right. It's our blood. And we stop at nothing. These buildings. They make us men. Eight hundred years we've studied here. We built this country. We made this nation. Darwin, Milton, Shadwell, Marlowe, Gladstone, Newton, Cromwell, Pitt. Then you. You what? Waltz in, with your bonnets and your pretentions and your preposterous self-belief and think you have a right to set foot in these walls? To put yourself on a level with us because you can heat a test tube on a burner? You know what they should do with you – they should put you away. You're mad. You're not natural. You don't have an ounce of womanhood in your body. You won't be mothers. And you won't be wives. Why would you do that? No normal woman would want that. Cos you know no man'll ever have you. You're a joke. All of you. A joke! Ha, a doctor, for God's sake! [...] Well, I'll be damned if any man would let you touch his body unless he's paying you like a common whore. ”

Brainstorm

Ned Glasier, Emily Lim and Company Three

TEN THINGS YOU NEED TO KNOW ABOUT YAAMIN:

- Yaamin is sixteen.
- He is one of several teenagers who have come to tell us about the workings of the teenage brain.

(Out of context, the following things are optional because the speech could be played by any sixteen-year-old boy.)

- He is Muslim.
- He comes from London.
- He lives with his mum Rana and baby sister Zara.
- Yaamin is trying to grow facial hair, but it's not really working out for him.
- Every morning before he leaves the house for college he goes to his mum's room and kisses her and baby sister on the forehead. In his culture the mother is the next important person after Allah or God.
- His mum is a social worker and driving instructor. When he is old enough, Yaamin wants to have free driving lessons, but his mum says that he if he doesn't get up in the morning he's going to have to pay for them himself.
- He has to do a lot of chores around the house and his mum screams at him if he is slack.
- He once had a massive fight with his mother because he bought the wrong kind of chicken from the supermarket.

FIVE THINGS TO HELP YOU PERFORM THE MONOLOGUE:

- You will need to read the entire play to understand fully the point that Yaamin is making. Throughout the play the audience are told about the workings of the teenage brain, and about how it develops. It is scientific and there is a lot of information that you need to absorb in order to perform the monologue well.

- The monologue comes at a pivotal point in the play, and in many ways expresses the feelings of all the other characters. Seen in this light, the speech becomes a kind of political statement on behalf of all misunderstood teenagers. It is passionate, honest and brave. See if you can capture the feeling of exhilaration when you finally dare to speak up for yourself.
- The speech is poetic. Notice the way it is written on the page, the way it is broken up as if it was a piece of poetry. See if you can find the rhythms within the text.
- Although Yaamin is fired up, there is also something sad about the lack of connection he feels towards his mother and the adult world in general. He is aware that they are growing apart, and there is something sorrowful about the tone of the speech, especially at the end when he goes lonely up to his room.
- Think about who he is talking to. On the one hand he is addressing the audience (see note on talking to the audience in the introduction), and on the other he is speaking specifically to his mother. See if you can imagine her reactions.

Yaamin

“You say to me

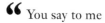

Your brain is broken.
It's like an adult's brain, but it doesn't work properly.

It's like you're in a city you've never been to and you don't have a map and you don't know what you're doing.
And you keep taking the wrong turns.

You say
Listen to me.
Don't worry.

One day you'll be okay.
Probably.
Your brain will start working properly.
One day your brain will be just like mine
And then you'll be okay.

But until then:
You've got to try and be more… like me.

I say to you
My brain isn't broken.
It's beautiful.

I'm in a city I've never been to and I see bright lights and new ideas and fear and opportunity and a thousand million roads all lit up and flashing.

I say
There are so many places to explore but you've forgotten that they exist because every day you walk the same way with your hands in your pockets and your eyes on the floor.

I say
When I'm wild and out of control
It's because I'm finding out who I am.

And if I was a real wild animal
Then I'd have left by now.

I say
My brain isn't broken
It's like this for a reason
I'm like this for a reason
I'm becoming who I am.

And I'm scared
And you're scared
Because who I am might not be who you want me to be.
Or who you are.

And I don't know why, but I *don't* say
It's all going to be okay.
There are so many things I stopped saying to you.

I want to say them
But I can't.

I pick up my plate
Put it in the kitchen
And go upstairs. ”

BU21

Stuart Slade

TEN THINGS YOU NEED TO KNOW ABOUT CLIVE:

- Clive is British Asian. The playwright has suggested that the actors swap the character names for their own names. You might prefer to do this. However, it is important that Clive has an English name because his parents were determined to assimilate into British culture.
- He is nineteen years old.
- Although his family are Muslim, they are secular (i.e. they do not practise their religion).
- They live in High Barnet in north London.
- Clive's father is a doctor, and Clive is studying for a law degree at Warwick University.
- He had wanted to do something else with his life, something less conventional, but in the end he caved in to family pressure.
- Clive and his dad argued a lot about religion, and whether, as Muslims, it was their duty to help other Muslims in Syria. Clive wanted to travel there, but his dad was totally against it.
- Because of their arguments Clive stopped speaking to his dad, and refused to come home in the holidays.
- Clive's dad died in a (fictional) terrorist attack when the plane he was travelling on came down in Fulham, west London. Five hundred and thirty-eight people died that day and over two thousand were injured.
- Clive is full of regret that he did not get to make it up with his dad before he died.

FIVE THINGS TO HELP YOU PERFORM THE MONOLOGUE:

- Clive is at a meeting for survivors of the BU21, the flight number of the aeroplane that crashed. Although there are other survivors in the room, he talks to us the audience (see note on talking to the audience in the introduction).
- You will need to connect to his feelings of grief and guilt. Although he himself was not harmed in the crash, he is at the meeting to try to make sense of his loss, and the terrible guilt he feels at not having spoken to his dad before he died.
- The speech is very funny. Underneath Clive is hurting, but on the surface he is covering his pain by trying to amuse or entertain us. See if you can capture these contradictory sensations.
- Clive has a very real identity crisis. How does it feel to be brought up English only to have the outside world regard you as a foreigner? Perhaps you too have experienced such prejudice.
- Clive asks the group to judge for themselves. Perhaps his main objective for attending the group is to seek forgiveness. Read the entire play to learn more about Clive.

N.B. This play offers several other monologues from which to choose.

Clive

“Hi. I'm Clive. Nice to meet you.

The trouble with stories is you never know how far to go back, do you, to make stuff make sense? Or is that just me?

Look – I'll just tell it from the very start so you can make your own decisions, okay?

So I was only like six or something when September 11th happened – and I literally had *no idea* what country New York was in, let alone who al-Qaeda were, or what jihadism was – but the next day – bang – I get punched in the face at school.

And I'm like – wow, what was that for?

Boy called Caius. Little shit. Classic class bully – you know? Thick neck, head like a football, bit like this – (*Mimes stupid face.*)

Probably in prison now –

Or a CEO or some shit, probably.

And from then on Caius called me 'Osama bin Clive'. Amazing mental journey he went on to reach that, you know?

And it was weird, because until then it hadn't *occurred* to me that there was even a *minimal* difference between me and everybody else in my class. We lived in the same sort of houses, our dads did the same sort of jobs, we watched the same stuff on TV, played with the same Transformers, everything. But after then, being a young Asian boy growing up in a mostly white area, every now and then – not *often*, I'm not trying to be whiney about it – but sometimes you're just like '*whoa* – are you actually being *serious*?' – especially after some terrorist shit's gone down recently.

I remember after the London Tube bombings when I was twelve – there was this *feeling*, you know? This *tension*.

Like all tension, though, you can kind of turn it to your advantage too? This one time, right, I was sitting on this packed bus next to a fat guy eating this really stinky skank-burger – it was really catching in my throat, like I was going to just vom on him –

So I just put my backpack on my lap –

And I close my eyes, put my hands out like this, and I start to mumble, like this – (*Mimes mouthing what sound like prayers.*)

Guy fucked off like a shot.

Whole seat for Clive, right there. Sweet as. Cheers, Osama.

So I wasn't even actually *praying* – that was the words to 'Bohemian Rhapsody' – Queen? (*Does it again – it is now clearly 'Bohemian Rhapsody'.*)

At that time I didn't even know any Muslim prayers.

Which was actually the other massive problem in my life. ”

Burying Your Brother in the Pavement

Jack Thorne

TEN THINGS YOU NEED TO KNOW ABOUT TIGHT:

- Tight is fourteen.
- He comes from an underprivileged background.
- He lives on a council estate. To the outside world the estate appears rough, but there is a strong sense of community and many people are happy there.
- Tight is a wheeler-dealer. He survives because he is streetwise.
- Tight is called 'Tight' because he is tight, as in 'not generous'.
- He is also described as 'kind of sweet'.
- Tight is gay.
- He was seeing a middle-class boy called Luke.
- When he broke up with Luke, Luke committed suicide.
- Tight is brave. Later on in the play, he will tell the police about their relationship and about how Luke killed himself.

FIVE THINGS TO HELP YOU PERFORM THE MONOLOGUE:

- Tight fancies himself as a bit of a wide boy, and has a kind of patter when he is trying to sell stuff. Think about the way he speaks – a bit 'gangster', a bit 'ghetto'.
- When Tight refers to 'the boy who got stabbed' he is talking about Luke. Luke killed himself by severing an artery in his neck with a smashed bottle. It has appeared as though he has been murdered. Notice the way Tight is distancing himself from the incident, as if he didn't know him. At this point in the play, he doesn't want people to find out that he is gay and that he has had a relationship with another boy.

- Imagine what Luke looks like. Perhaps you have had a relationship with someone that you later dumped. How did it make you feel? Relieved or guilty? After Luke's suicide, Tight feels responsible.
- Tight is talking to Tom, a 'posh' boy who is not from the estate. See if you can picture what he looks like. Tom is a geek and is described as 'uncool'. Think about how you are trying to protect him. (Later on in the scene Tight will discover that Tom is Luke's brother.)
- The monologue is very funny and you can have fun playing it. In the original text some of it is conversation between Tight and Tom that I have edited to make it flow like one speech. It is important that you find the rhythm so that the speech has a kind of 'bounce' to it, as though there is some movement back and forth. Picture Tom's reactions, and in your head listen to what he's just asked or said to you.

Tight

“You wanna buy a Travelcard? […] I got some Travelcards, you wanna buy one? […] Give you great price? […] I ain't a generous guy normal. I am known round here as 'Tight' cos I'm like… tight. But for you – my business associates would literally kill me for this – but I could be prepared – on this occasion, and on this occasion only, to give wholesale prices, just cos – well – you look like a kid who just got given a teddy and realised it's full of used syringes and condoms – […] You sure about the Travelcard? […] This ain't the place for a boy like you. Take a Travelcard, go somewhere better. I mean, boy 'bout your age got stabbed here less than a week ago. With a bottle. You know what I'm saying? […] I mean, you is in Tunstall land now, this place is the definition of rough – look rough up in your dictionary, you'd get a photo of this place. I mean, we is basically sitting on a murder scene here, serious! This area supposed to have all dem 'police don't cross' signs and stuff round it. Yellow tape you know, with the black stripes, looks pretty cool, yeah? But someone nicked it. That's how dangerous this area is – we don't just get told we're dangerous, we nick the tape that tells us it. Rah! […] You don't want any 'police don't cross' yellow tape, do you? Cos I just happened to come into a little bit of it myself recently. Very good price. ”

Burying Your Brother in the Pavement

Jack Thorne

TEN THINGS YOU NEED TO KNOW ABOUT TOM:

- Tom is in his early teens.
- He comes from a middle-class background and is described as 'posh'.
- He comes from London, but out of context he could come from any part of the country.
- He lives with his mum and dad, and older sister Courtney.
- His older brother Luke has died recently. It has appeared as though he has been murdered.
- Tom hated his brother.
- Tom is very clever and when he was moved up a year at school and put into his brother's class, it put a real strain on their relationship.
- Tom is a geek and is uncool.
- His only friend is a boy called Martin. They are in the computer club together.
- Although Tom is shy, he is also very brave. Read the whole play to find out what really happened to Luke and how Tom deals with his grief.

FIVE THINGS TO HELP YOU PERFORM THE MONOLOGUE:

- This monologue comes at the very start of the play. Tom is talking to the audience (see note on talking to the audience in the introduction). He is hiding under a table in a large dusty attic. You might like to start the speech under the table, but then come out as soon as you feel the speech is becoming too static. If you are using the speech for an audition, you may decide that it is simpler to do without it altogether.

- Tom is enjoying the attention and likes to entertain us. Although his brother has just died, what he says is very funny. It might help to think of it as a piece of stand-up comedy.
- When really bad things happen to people, they go into shock. It could be that Tom hasn't fully comprehended the enormity of the situation. This may explain why he doesn't appear upset. You can also factor in the truth about their relationship – that he and his brother did not get on.
- When you perform the monologue, think about what you will wear to show that you are uncool and a 'geek'. It says in the stage directions that Tom is wearing his brother's 'cool' clothes, but in a really 'uncool' way.
- Think about how Tom likes to overdramatise things, like believing that he is the son of God or dying of AIDS. Does your imagination ever play tricks with you like this? Do you ever pretend that you are super-human or that you might catch some terrible disease? Explore ways of connecting to this kind of self-centredness.

Tom

" I first had the idea that I was the son of God, when I was nine.

I'd just read the Bible.

Not the whole Bible, not cover-to-cover but – you know… extensive dipping… Anyway, the more I read, the more it sort of made sense, that I was the second coming. Jesus Christ. Two.

The sequel.

I mean, my mum a virgin? Well, looking at her you could certainly believe so. Check. Dad not my real dad? We never did have much in common. Check. Me leading a sad-and-tortured-life-where-everyone-hates-me-and-I-have-to-die-for-the-good-of-humanity-who'll-be-sorry-when-I'm-gone?

Check.

But then I tried to cure a leper – well, a kid with really bad eczema… it didn't work. He just bled a lot. I tried to – rip some of his skin off and…

Beat.

I first got the idea I might have AIDS after a particularly aggressive sex-ed class – you know, the sort of class where your teacher just repeatedly shouts – […]

'You must NEVER have sex. Never. Ever. Ever.'

I mean, talk about premature, I hadn't even persuaded a girl to kiss me yet. But he always was premature, Mr Wilkins. […] So AIDS – me? Unlikely! But then I had a tetanus shot and it took them ages to find a vein and I thought – well, maybe I had a mutated version of AIDS – the sort where you don't get to do anything good to catch it. 'I caught mine through drugs.' 'I caught mine through sex.' 'I just, well, I just sort of got it.' 'Why?' 'Because I'm unlucky.'

There are loads of other examples – the time I thought I'd developed a cure for blindness in biology class because I seemed to be able to see things with my eyes closed – the time when I thought I may have inadvertently started a war between Korea and the Isle of Sheppey with some stuff I'd written on my blog – the time when I thought I'd accidentally castrated my dog –

Okay, well, I sort of did castrate my dog. That's a long story… my point is this…

It's normal to be centre of your own world, in your head, star of your… and me… I don't just star in my head, I kind of suffocate all other forms of life. But this – finally – I've got the opportunity to actually be some kind of star and I'm – […]

They're a – having a funeral downstairs.

I'm supposed to be there. Down there. With them.

I mean, it's not like a guy missing his own wedding – I mean, it's not my funeral, obviously – TA-DAH! I'm alive – so, but… still… I'm expected to be there. And not here – hiding under a table in my attic.

He chews a finger and looks contemplative.

Luke – my brother – always used to come up here when he was upset. I was – too afraid – always thought there was something living up here. Something swimming in the water tank, sliding through the pipes, nestling in the insulation. But now – well –

Funerals – fun-e-rals – rals from the Latin meaning 'the rule is'. The rule… is fun. Great news for my little cousin Kevin, who has jam around his mouth and mayonnaise in his hair and likes randomly launching into his world-famous impression of Robbie Williams. And less good news for my mum who just wants to cry – on me. […]

My brother died. Badly. It's that simple really…

He chews a finger and looks contemplative.

You know why they call them wakes? It used to be a time when people sat by the body waiting to see if it woke up. Before doctors knew what they were doing. Some bodies did wake up – in which case they were alive and mourning was kind of pointless – others didn't – in which case… well… Either way, everyone got drunk.

I know that I can't stay here. I didn't mean to – I was panicked up here when an auntie I barely knew, licked my face and told me I was a good boy and then tried to give me a deep-fried-mushroom thing from Iceland. And it…

Jesus didn't have to deal with this rubbish, did he? ❞

Chatroom

Enda Walsh

TEN THINGS YOU NEED TO KNOW ABOUT JIM:

- Jim is fifteen years old.
- He comes from Chiswick in west London.
- He describes himself as 'very skinny and a bit funny looking'.
- He lives with his mother, who is a single parent, and his three older brothers.
- Other kids describe his mother as 'a social climber with ideas above her station'.
- Jim struggles to fit in. With three beefy older brothers, he is the runt of the family.
- Jim's father walked out on the family when Jim was only six. Jim's father went missing when he took Jim on a trip to the zoo. His mum and older brothers were away that weekend, and Jim's dad was supposed to be looking after him. Jim had to make his own way home.
- On some level, Jim blames himself for his father's disappearance, and the whole experience has left him traumatised.
- Jim was bullied throughout primary school, and this has continued into his secondary school, where he is not popular and the girls don't fancy him.
- Jim is depressed, even suicidal.

FIVE THINGS TO HELP YOU PERFORM THE MONOLOGUE:

- Jim has joined a suicide chatroom to talk about his depression. He's not sure it's that serious yet, but he clearly needs to offload. In the monologue that follows, he is talking to Laura, also fifteen. She doesn't offer advice, she just listens. When you perform the monologue you might like to imagine talking into a void. In reality, Jim would be typing into a computer, but the theatrical convention has all the characters sitting in a line on plastic chairs. He wouldn't know what Laura looks like, which probably allows him to feel safe.

- Key to Jim's depression is the disappearance of his father. Although this speech starts off being about something else, it is obvious that it is related. You will need to be clear from the outset that your reason for recounting this episode has to do with explaining the source of your depression.
- The monologue itself is very funny. However, it is the kind of humour that the speaker may not be aware of. See if you can strike a balance between Jim's depression and the 'dark' comedy of what he is describing.
- The monologue mentions a lot of people in Jim's life. You will need to have very clear pictures in your mind's eye of everyone that you mention.
- The monologue is quite long, and it needs to be played at a good pace. Without rushing it, see if you can find an urgency about it. Remember that Jim really needs to talk and all this is spilling out of him.

Jim

" I'm a Roman Catholic… and it's last Easter… and ahhh… and every year our parish does a big Passion play in our local church. My mother's very active in the church. She's the Virgin Mary. […] In the Passion play she's the Virgin Mary. […] And my whole family get involved. I've got three older brothers and they're Roman soldiers. They're very broad… not like me… and they look the part. One year my brother Derek went too heavy on Jesus and actually popped his knee right open. It was a mess. But anyway, this year and my mother runs into my bedroom with her 'terrific news'. She's building it up like she's going to tell me that I'm going to get a stab at playing a centurion… until she tells me… they want me to play John. [...] Yeah, but he's a bit gay. [...] I've got nothing against gay people. [...] Historically speaking, he probably wasn't gay. But in our parish it's always the slightly effeminate boys who get to play John. [...] Like I say... I've got nothing against gays. I respect the gay community. They're tough, they know their own mind, they stand out and they don't care, you know. I respect them. But I'm not like that at all. I'm just a sap with no bottle who knows nothing. I'm not interesting enough to play the gay icon that is St John. In a million years I could never get away with those lime robes. [...] It's sort of an unspoken thing in the parish. It's a bit weird. [...] We do a few rehearsals with my mother as the Virgin Mary and I've got to get emotional when Jesus is dying on the cross and he says to Mary, 'Woman, behold your son,' while looking over at me. And I'm supposed to break down at that point because I know that Jesus is just about to croak it but I'm getting very nervous because basically I'm a terrible actor and I'm all blocked up. [...] So I tell my mother I want to drop out of the play. I say it quiet so the others can't hear but she starts screaming at me and saying how typical it was... and did I have a backbone?... and why was I such a coward?... and why wasn't I like my older brothers... and all this shit. And then she says I'm like my dad. But what would I know?... I haven't seen my dad since I was six... but she starts shouting, 'You're just like your dad, Jim!... Just like your dad, walking out on things! Walking out on me! Gutless!' I mean, I hate her just then. Why did she have to bring up my dad in front of all of those people like that. Why?! So the following night is the Passion play proper and I'm kneeling and looking up at Jesus. He's doing a wonderful job dying on the cross, this guy called Nick Lawson. He's into amateur dramatics in a big way... I actually saw him in a production of *Babes in the Wood* playing the Widow Twankey and I swear to God he was hilarious... but as Jesus Christ he was even better... obviously not in a hilarious way but... [...] Right. So Nick's line to me and my mother is coming up and I'm still really furious with her from the night before. 'Woman, behold your son,' cries Nick. (*Pause.*) At the start I didn't know whether it was his great delivery or just thinking about my mother being my mother… but I started to cry. I'm crying really hard. People are thinking that this is wonderful. I completely upstage Nick's crucifixion and the night's suddenly about St John and whether he's going to be all right and if he'll have the strength to carry on and start and finish his gospel. But anyway! Anyway! Afterwards and my mother is having a lemonade in the sacristy and I'm out of my lime robes and looking over at her. And I realise why I was crying back then. (*Pause.*) I was crying because I know my mother doesn't like me. (*Pause.*) If I really remind her of the man she hates, the man who left us when I was six… then maybe I should walk away too. But where to? Where do I go to? ”

Cressida

Nicholas Wright

TEN THINGS YOU NEED TO KNOW ABOUT HONEY:

- Honey is eighteen.
- He lives and works in London in the early seventeenth-century theatre.
- He is what is known as 'a boy actor': because women were not allowed to appear on stage at that time, the boy actors played all the female parts.
- He is a well-respected and admired player.
- Titania from Shakespeare's *A Midsummer Night's Dream* is one of his finest roles.
- He is on the cusp of manhood, and because his voice might break at any point, he knows that his career is in the balance.
- He is worldly wise and savvy.
- He is flirtatious and a bit of a tart.
- He has relationships with men and women.
- He likes to smoke opium.

FIVE THINGS YOU NEED TO PERFORM THE MONOLOGUE:

- Honey is talking to Stephen, a fourteen-year-old 'would-be' boy actor. Honey knows Stephen to be a terrible actor, but nevertheless a potential rival. Perhaps there is someone with whom you are competitive, so you can connect to that feeling of wanting to prove yourself better. Honey wants to intrigue and to impress Stephen. He is also toying with him.
- Because Honey knows that his career is coming to an end, the monologue is a chance to reflect on his own success, to savour his moment of glory and to rest in its glow. See if you can connect to that feeling of knowing something is ending

and wanting to enjoy every last drop or moment. Perhaps it's a bit like the final day of a holiday, when you soak up that last bit of sun and relaxation before getting on a plane back home.

- Honey is high from smoking opium. I do not suggest that you play 'stoned', but you can decide to what extent Honey's vivid description is born out of this altered state.
- The 'Jhon' to whom he refers is the boy's dresser.
- It would greatly help to familiarise yourself with early seventeenth-century theatre practice and to read Nicholas Wright's Afterword at the back of the playtext.

Honey

" It's different at different times. [...] Well, when you're young, you're just a child being clever. Then it changes. [...] When you get older. When other boys get tall and clumsy. And their voices drop two million pegs. We don't do that. We hang on. [...] We just do. It's like a baby falling down a well. You've got its foot in your hand and you don't let go. So you're not one thing exactly. You're half-man, half-boy. That's when you find you can really do it. And it's amazing. It's better than beer or wine. It's better than smoking. It's like flying. It's like finding that wings have suddenly sprouted from your shoulders. You come on stage and everything happens the way it's meant to. And nobody in the audience looks at anyone else. Because you live in a sort of stolen time that they can't get to. Except through you. And it could disappear at any moment. You're like a soldier on the eve of battle. Every night could be your last. And everyone wants to be that special person on that special night. That's my theory. That's why they grab old Jhon, J, H, O, N, and give him notes for us. It's why they hang about at the Actors' Door.

He puts out the pipe, starts getting out of his dress.

I still get letters every day. Not just from men. Everyone thinks I'm just a boyish bugger. That's not true. I see women as well. They're even stranger than the men are. They ask me to supper and want me to bring my gown and make-up.

He stands, the gown in his arms.

Take it.

We'll carry them back to Shanky. He'll pay his debt to the Board and you'll stay on. Isn't that what you wanted? ❞

Crushed Shells and Mud

Ben Musgrave

TEN THINGS YOU NEED TO KNOW ABOUT DEREK:

- Derek is seventeen.
- He lives in a small seaside village on the east coast of England.
- He is sensitive and kind, but also awkward and shy.
- He likes to write stories and poetry.
- He loves nature and the sea.
- He spends much of his time in a disused caravan in a field near the sea. It is his den.
- He loves music from the 1990s and makes up his own compilations.
- He steers clear of alcohol, smoking and drugs.
- Derek doesn't socialise in the evenings – he has to go home to make the tea.
- In the play, there is a deadly disease that is gripping the nation. It has ravaged London and is making its way up the coast.

FIVE THINGS TO HELP YOU PERFORM THE MONOLOGUE:

- This speech comes close to the start of the play. It is actually a conversation between Derek and Lydia (although Derek does most of the talking). It works well as a monologue as long as you give a little time to imagine Lydia's responses. For clarity, I have put Lydia's lines in square brackets. I would suggest saying them as if you are repeating back to her what she has just said to you.
- See if you can get an image in your head of what Lydia looks like. Derek is described as 'not in her league'. It is clear from the monologue, that even though they have only just met, he is already in love with her.

- Think about the way he speaks. He will have an accent of some sort. Out of context, any accent that is rural or not from the city would work.
- He is awkward with Lydia. He is naturally shy, and because he so obviously fancies her he might sound a bit too eager or clumsy. See if you can capture this quality.
- Take time to imagine your environment. See if you can picture the caravan, and the overgrown path to the sea. What does it feel like to be outside? Imagine you can hear the sound of the sea.

Derek

" (*Of the path to the sea.*) Now, normally you can get to the sea this way, there's a path that winds down, but there haven't been the walkers really, in recent years.
So it's quite grown over.

I'll see if I can beat it back at the weekend. [...]

Oh I don't mind! [...]

We need to keep it open.
It's a right of way.
You can't just let it go.

(*Of the caravan.*) This is just...

Someone just dumped this here.
We use it sometimes – the farmer doesn't mind.

You're most welcome at any time. [...]

DEREK *tries to point out the view.*

Well, that's the sea.

(*Looking down into the vegetation.*) It's not a great beach, if I'm honest.
Quite muddy.
There's a better one further down the coast.
Rockpools, a bit of sand.

I could show you? […]

I'm not much of a swimmer.
Well, I can thrash about…

(*Of her name.*) It was 'Lydia' wasn't it? […]

(*Embarrassed.*) I always forget in the flurry of it.
And then it's embarrassing to ask again.

Pause.

(*Of his name.*) Derek. […]

Did you swim where you were before? […]

Where was it?

Beat.

[Sussex.]

So this must be a bit of a change! […]

Everything okay there? […]

Your parents move out here? […]

[They're in…

Germany.]

(*Of the whole area.*) There's not much here.

It's not
Well it's not too wonderful.

If you're after clubs and things there's one in Stonesea. We had a disco at the village hall last year but it wasn't up to much.

There's a shop or two and a pub.

I think it would be hard in a new place. […]

I don't know I'd have the bravery to be honest.

Don't worry, you'll be alright. You'll be as right as rain!

Pause. He can think of only one solution.

I can do you a cup of tea?

Pause.

(*Of the caravan.*) I've got a thing rigged up in here. [...]

Maybe you have to go? [...]

Right!
I'll go and get it on.
(*Of the tea.*) It might have to be black I'm afraid. ”

Crushed Shells and Mud

Ben Musgrave

TEN THINGS YOU NEED TO KNOW ABOUT VINCENT:

- Vincent in seventeen.
- He lives in a small seaside village on the east coast of England.
- He is smart in a way that 'Derek' (see previous monologue) is not.
- He is a bully.
- He deals drugs, supplying other kids with weed.
- He comes from an abusive home, and we know that his father is not a nice man.
- He and Derek have been friends since childhood.
- He, like Derek, fancies Lydia.
- Unlike Derek, he is sexually confident and has none of Derek's awkwardness.
- In the play, there is a deadly disease that is gripping the nation. It has ravaged London and is making its way up the coast.

FIVE THINGS TO HELP YOU PERFORM THE MONOLOGUE:

- Vincent is cruel. On the one hand he says he is protecting Derek, but on the other he seems to delight in putting him down. See if you can capture his 'superior' tone. By going on about how great sex with Lydia will be he's really rubbing Derek's nose in it.
- What makes a bully like Vincent? Rather than judge him, think about how he has learned this kind of behaviour. There is the suggestion in the play that Vincent's father has been violent and abusive.
- See if you can imagine what both Derek and Lydia look like. Read the whole play to get a fuller picture.

- Think about the way he speaks. There is a roughness about him, and he will have an accent of some sort. Out of context, any accent that is rural or not from the city would work.
- Think about how Vincent's toughness is like a kind of armour that he puts on to protect himself. How might he stand? What is his overall physicality like and how does it differ from Derek's? You might like to wear a leather or denim jacket when you perform the speech to give you that feeling of strength.

Vincent

" Just be careful, mate. [...]

I don't want you to get hurt.
I don't want you to think 'oh things are going pretty well for me' when they're not.

Is that what you think?
'I'm quietly confident.'
This new girl with the sweetest breath in England, she turns up and for some reason, for a few moments, she's showing you some interest.

It's a mistake, Derek.
It's a mistake that awkward shy boys have made throughout history.
When everything is up in the air, when everything's new, this kind of girl they can sometimes make mistakes. Jumble people up.
Get trapped with the wrong company.

And the longer they're trapped the more vicious the snap will be. [...]

Your goodness won't turn her on.
It'll just make her feel terrible.

Pause.

I'm going to fuck her, Derek.
I just know it. It's like destiny.

I will.
I'll fuck her and there'll be fireworks all over London.
That's what I'm going to do. [...]

Of course, I know there must be some 'thing' about her.
There's always some 'thing' about girls like her.
With a reason to be shy.
Is she the girl who gets addicted?
Or doesn't like to eat.
Or hides the cuts on her arms?

I don't care.
I don't care about any of that stuff.

Pause.

Are we still friends, Derek? ”

Dean McBride*

Sonya Hale

TEN THINGS YOU NEED TO KNOW ABOUT DEAN:

- Dean is sixteen.
- He lives on a council estate outside Croydon in south-east London.
- He lives with his dad who is an alcoholic. His dad is not well, and by the end of the play he will have died.
- Dean's mother, who is a recovering drug addict, left home when he was little. She has tried to reconnect with Dean, but he has rejected her.
- In many ways, Dean has been forced to grow up too soon. He is the one who takes care of his dad, not the other way around.
- Dean has a tough outer shell, but on the inside he is sensitive and vulnerable.
- Although he didn't enjoy school, he is good at maths.
- Dean's passion is football. He and his dad support Crystal Palace.
- His best friend is called Marve. They like to hang out in the local car park, smoking weed and chatting up girls.
- Dean is in love with a girl called Lilly.

FIVE THINGS TO HELP YOU PERFORM THE MONOLOGUE:

- This speech forms part of a much longer monologue which makes up a whole play. It is one of the funnier and more tender moments. See if you can capture Dean's 'loved-up-ness' – he says he can't eat or sleep. Perhaps you have felt a similar attraction and you know that sensation of feeling out of

* Published in the volume *Heretic Voices*

control. Read the whole play to see how it contrasts with Dean's behaviour when he is with his dad, mum or Marve.

- There is something special about Lilly. We know she has amazing dark eyes and that she wears a blue dress and has a yellow rucksack. See if you can really picture her in your mind's eye and make those colours very vivid in your imagination.
- Dean speaks with a multicultural-London-English accent, or MLE. It has a particular musicality and features many slang terms. You can also hear a version of it in Manchester and Birmingham. If this accent or way of speaking is not native/familiar to you, you will need to study it in order to perform the speech.
- Think about how Lilly speaks and how Dean impersonates her when he is recounting their conversations. Perhaps her voice is sweet and mellow. See how far you can go in your impression of Lilly. It could be quite funny.
- Think about your relationship to the audience (see note on talking to the audience in the introduction). If you are not actually performing the monologue in front of a real audience, think about who they might be. For instance, are they people of your own age, other boys perhaps or are they adults? How does it change the tone of the speech if you imagine you are talking to a particular kind of group? And given the fact that Dean appears comfortable confiding in the audience, what do you think works best for the speech?

NB This play offers several other monologues from which to choose.

Dean

" I've got this rare-up job now in Tesco, Portland Road, sweet – I mean it's nothing special but pay's okay and means I can tear up weekends and as soon as I get the job I'm straight on the till, straight in, boss loves me, beat all the other kiddies on account of being so goddamn quick – boss says my maths is blaze and I'm 'reliable, dependable,' he says. Chief. Pisser, but he's kinda right I am kinda blaze… and I is all like charm bwoy, butter them shoppers – old ladies and shit, bare jokes then one day when the boss is on errand, me and this other kiddy we've got run of the shop and my man is flass – chucking grapes – catching them in his mouth and I am juggling fruit, I'm chucking these plums up high in the air, I got skills bwoy, nearly touch the ceiling and we got the whole queue in stitches – (*Beat.*) When I see her – I spot her by the tins of kidney beans, stood there, twiddling her hair, smiling… And I drop my plums. They all come tumbling down around me and this woman claps. I don't know where to put my eyes. I can feel my skin tight like I am transparent or some shit and I'm burning up now bwoy – shit, shit… I want to run away but the kiddy I'm with says…

'Can we help you madam?' He is chief.

But she don't look at him she just keeps looking at me – grinning so much and she is so goddamn pretty. She's got these dark eyes and this little blue dress on and her eyes are sparkling! She reaches to the floor and picks up one of my plums and hands it to me – 'You dropped this.' She says. Giggling… 'They're proper nice and squishy…' And I think oh my days like I have arrived bwoy!

Sweat gushing but I don't give a shit –

'Oi, gormo…' My man nudges me but I –

Beat.

'Thank you.' I say and she –

'My name's Lilly.' And I cough and 'Hello… My name's – ' and I fucking start telling her all what my name is and how I live up the road and this is my job and when I've finished she says, 'And can I?' I don't know what she fucking means –

'Can I?' (*Beat.*) And she takes the plum and bites it and 'Mmmm… It *is* juicy….' she says grinning…

I don't see her for a whole week then, a whole fucking week – 'gallie nicked my plums' I laugh but it ain't no jokes – I can't sleep, can't eat and then I think I'll never find her but then after six long hard-core days I see her out on the street, with the same blue dress and a little yellow rucksack, pacing and she's looking in the window, looking for me. Our eyes meet – shit! I have to go see her now, say hello. 'Oi – ' I say to ma bwoy, 'Cover me innit?' And I rush out onto the street –

Beat.

'Hello…' I say and 'Do you need anything? Do you need some shopping? We've got some proper nice produce in.' And I feel like *such a dick* but she just keeps smiling, she says 'I brought you this' and she hands me a fruit salad medley. 'Sainsbury's, feel like a bit of a traitor innit?' And I take it and we giggle a bit. I ask her what fruit she likes, 'Pineapple,' she says and I say 'I like mango,' and she tells me she ate mango once, straight from the tree in Sierra Leone where her dad is living, she picked it from the tree when she went to visit. She tells me how the juice drips sweet in the heat, 'Like nectar,' she says and I can like flipping taste it. 'Fuck Croydon mangos!' She gives it – 'I'd rather munch on bricks!' 'Not everything in Croydon tastes like shit,' I say, 'Some of us are tasty.' And she pushes me… (*Smiles.*) ❞

The Distance

Deborah Bruce

This monologue contains language that some people might find offensive.

TEN THINGS YOU NEED TO KNOW ABOUT LIAM:

- Liam is fifteen.
- He comes from Peckham in south-east London, and is one of those middle-class kids who lives in a predominantly working-class area.
- He lives with his mum, Alex, who is a single parent. She has had three sons, all by different fathers.
- Liam's own father shows no interest in him, and while the other boys spend time with their dads, Liam is often alone.
- Alex is not very responsible. She drinks too much, and Liam has to fend for himself. Perhaps because of this, rather than rebel, Liam has to be sensible.
- Although technically he comes from a 'broken home', Liam is well-adjusted.
- Liam is chatty.
- Liam has suffered from asthma.
- Liam plays the oboe.
- He says that the best ten days of his life were when he went on an outward bound course with a friend of his. They slept in a tent and learnt how to survive in the wild.

FIVE THINGS TO HELP YOU PERFORM THE MONOLOGUE:

- Liam is talking to Bea, a friend of his mother's. She has just walked out on her husband and two sons in Australia, and is quizzing Liam about whether he feels 'damaged' because of the way his (Liam's) dad has behaved. Perhaps you can imagine you are talking to a friend of *your* mother's, or perhaps there is a teacher at school that you could picture. Whoever you choose, make sure you have a clear idea in your head about what Bea looks like, and before you start the speech imagine you are responding to her question, 'Do you ever think about your dad?' I have inserted the line 'My dad?' in square brackets at the top of the speech for clarification.

- In order for the punchline 'what a cunt' to work, the rest of the speech should be tender and even wistful. Remember that Liam plays the oboe. His speech has something lyrical about it and could be played much like a beautiful piece of music.
- Do not rush the speech. Liam is responding to a question and is thinking as he speaks. He gets very into the idea of synchronicity, and there is an intensity and focus about him.
- See if you can really picture all the everyday objects that he describes – the phone, the drink, the sandwich, the TV remote and the glass. What are you imagining is in the sandwich? What sort of bread is it? How does it taste? The more you can bring these details to life the better.
- How might Liam imagine his father to look? Is the image a distant one from memory, or has he a photograph on which to base his idea? We do know that his father moved to Brazil, remarried and then got divorced. However, when Alex tried to contact him, he failed to reply.

Liam

“ [My dad?] Sometimes. Not really. […] I dunno […] Sometimes, I think, like, you know when something happens to you and like it happens to your mate at the same time? You know like if you get a text message at exactly the same time that your mate's phone gets a text. And your phone's like, beep beep, and his phone's like, beep beep, at the exact same time and you're like, oh my God, that's such a coincidence? Or like you both go into a shop and you get split up but when you come out you've got like the exact same stuff? The same drink, or whatever.[…] Sometimes I think that. You know. That's weird but what about all the times when that happens but you *don't even know*. How weird is *that*? Like sometimes if I'm like biting into a sandwich or whatever, and I think, what if, you know, my dad was like biting into a sandwich at like, the exact same time? Or like, the same kind of sandwich? Or like when I put the TV on standby before I go to bed and the house is really quiet and then I think, you know, as I take like a step or move my hand to like, pick up my glass, wouldn't it be weird if like, me and my dad were moving at exactly the same time, at the same speed, like synchronised swimmers but not even knowing. Sometimes I think that. […]

Pause.

And other times I think, you know, what a cunt! […]

But mostly, I don't think about him at all. ”

Epic Love and Pop Songs

Phoebe Eclair-Powell

TEN THINGS YOU NEED TO KNOW ABOUT TED:

- Ted is sixteen.
- He is highly sensitive, honest and compassionate.
- The bullies at school call him a 'freak' and a 'wet weirdo', and he struggles to fit in.
- Ted's parents are separated.
- He lives with his dad.
- He had an older sister called Bethany, but she was murdered when she was sixteen.
- After the murder, his mother went to live in Spain.
- Ted's only friend is a wild girl called Doll. Although she can be violent, Ted can see the side of Doll that needs looking after.
- Doll has faked a pregnancy in order to get attention. But the plan has backfired and the other girls at school have become even more hostile. When they find out that there is no baby, Doll will be humiliated. Ted wants to protect Doll from having to suffer the shame that his sister did.
- The playwright describes Ted as a 'hero'. Read the whole play to find out what happens to Ted and Doll.

FIVE THINGS TO HELP YOU PERFORM THE MONOLOGUE:

- Ted is talking to the audience (see note on talking to the audience in the introduction). Doll has insisted he tell us about what happened to Bethany because she wants him to admit that his real reason for protecting her, Doll, is that he was unable to protect Bethany. To a large extent this is true.
- You will need to have a very good image in your head about what Doll and Bethany look like, as well as all the other characters that he mentions.

- The play is a two-hander between Doll and Ted. This speech comes quite close to the end. Although it must be painful to recall, to what extent might it be a relief for Ted to finally tell us all this?
- Consider the myriad of confused emotions he must feel. He was only a little boy when his sister was murdered, and it certainly wasn't his fault. Yet he still feels a kind of guilt and shame at not having protected his sister. Furthermore, he has had to cope with the separation of his parents, missing his mum and the attacks from those around who should be sympathetic.
- As you chart your way through the monologue, make sure you are very clear about what you are thinking and feeling. There's a lot there, from love for your sister, an attraction and then anger directed at Julia, through to horror and shock at what happened, a helplessness, and then loneliness at losing your mum, and finally, a rage with the outside world. Bring all this detail to your performance and remember to be specific.

Ted

“My sister was sixteen when it happened, which is how old we are now.

She was tall for her age and really, really fit.

She had eyes that were bolt-stripe blue and eyelashes that looked like adverts.

She loved our cousin Julia more than anything and Julia was eighteen and had tits that I couldn't stop dreaming about which I know isn't quite right, but, trust me I can't stop thinking about most people's tits, so maybe it wasn't too incestuous… maybe.

Julia lent my sister everything, make-up, shoes, the skirt she was wearing and her vodka.

Julia didn't go home with my sister that night and most of the family still won't talk to her because of it. You see she let

Bethany go off with these random men, boys, who knows, the CCTV isn't very clear you see – just blurs and she's gone, like that. And there's nothing more but the broken bones they found a week later. There's not even a glimmer of bolt-stripe blue you can see in her eyes and they won't let my mum identify her – upsetting apparently. So I never really got to see what she looked like. But I see her every time I close my eyes.

Mum couldn't live with us any more after it happened, sort of coped and then just sort of flipped it, one day the paper had Bethany's picture on it, all the papers did, and it was one from school, skirt rolled up and her hair down – none of it allowed and she looked like a right slag, my sister, she had her tongue out and her piercing looked like a bit of printing gone wrong. Mum shuddered and remembered fighting with her about that, threatening to 'pull the fucking thing out because it would probably just get infected'. Mum came home with a stack of *Sun*s and *Echo*es and burnt them all in a mess in the garden. Then went upstairs into her room and started dry retching, heaving, shouting 'I can't get it out'. My dad took her paper-black hands and wrapped himself around her, told me to 'get her passport, son, be a good lad'.

She lives with Uncle Stanley who only has one leg – gout ate the other one – in a pub on a port near Marbella and she is beginning to slowly be, not happy, but normal. She sends us postcards of dancers with frilly bits that stick out, they never say very much.

[...]

In my sleep I see my sister climbing over a fence she shouldn't have climbed with the men she shouldn't have trusted and I think about the voicemail she left me – 'cover for me' was all it said and I didn't want her to be blamed any more than she already had been.

Don't you get it, Doll – I didn't want them to do to you, what they did to her.

I'm not letting that happen, the faces and the laughing, Samantha Hogan putting it on Facebook and no one ever,

ever, ever forgetting. Her name and number all over the boys' toilets, the way they talk about her – the ones who slept with her acting like it makes them special. The next-door neighbours tutting like they knew it would happen. Like she had it coming. The whole school still posting pictures of Bethany all over my profile like it's nothing. Like I don't see her walking down the stairs every morning. Fucktards the lot of them. Fucking fuck… shit.

What were you thinking, Doll? ”

The Ferryman

Jez Butterworth

TEN THINGS YOU NEED TO KNOW ABOUT DIARMAID:

- The year is 1981.
- Diarmaid is sixteen.
- He comes from Derry in Northern Ireland.
- He is a Roman Catholic.
- He likes the music of the time such as punk band The Undertones.
- He lives with his parents and his two brothers Shane and Declan.
- His older brother, Shane, has been groomed by the Irish Republican Army.
- Diarmaid is often a figure of fun. Both Shane and younger brother Declan regard him as a bit of a fool.
- Diarmaid can be boisterous, but he is also a natural peacemaker. If there is the threat of a fight he would rather smooth things over.
- Diarmaid is essentially soft and kind. He lacks his older brother's gift for telling a story and his younger brother's piercing tongue.

FIVE THINGS TO HELP YOU PERFORM THE MONOLOGUE:

- Firstly you will need to familiarise yourself with Northern Irish politics of the late 1970s and early '80s – 'The Troubles' – and in particular with the imprisoned members of the Irish Republican Army who went on hunger strike to further their cause. Bobby Sands refused to eat for sixty-six days before dying at the age of twenty-seven.
- The speech is made up of a conversation that Diarmaid and his two brothers (the Corcoran boys) are having with their

country cousins, the Carney boys. In many ways, the Carney boys have been sheltered from the bitter and dirty feud between the Catholics and Protestants in Northern Ireland, and the Corcoran boys are enjoying showing off. See if you can picture their reactions as you tell what happened.

- You will need to find a contrast between what is funny and what is serious. Diarmaid starts off telling the 'story' to illicit laughs, but then by the time he talks about the RA men (the IRA) his tale takes on a more sinister tone and he is looking for a different reaction. He is still showing off but, lacking his older brother's 'gift of the gab', he fumbles the punchline. See if you can try to build to a really important moment, only to forget the last important bit.
- The monologue is rich in visual detail and takes in a number of different people and locations. Use your imagination to picture all that he describes.
- Notice the stage direction '*swigs again*'. The boys, who have spent the day bringing in the harvest, are drinking whiskey, so you might like to try the speech whilst taking swigs from a bottle (see note on using props in the introduction). However, be careful that you don't overplay drunk. At this stage in the conversation Diarmaid is more merry and energetic than 'out of it' or tired.

Diarmaid

“We got the first bus from Waterside and it's coming down stair rods all the way. 6 a.m. and the coach is sardines, we're stood up all the way, riding into Belfast on the way to the funeral. The driver's got the radio on full-blast and your man there's sayin' eighty, ninety thousand folk are lining the street. The bus is red-hot, steamed up, dripping down the windows. Banners, flags, all furled, but we haven't got no flag nor banner, all we've got is a fuckin' Bic. This Bic biro. Right? So I take it and write your man's name on my hand. And Shane writes it on his. 'Bobby Sands. RIP.' And we write it on the back of our jackets. But the fucking biro packs in. The nib breaks. All it says on my back is 'BO'. [...] I'm gonna walk around all day with 'BO' on my back. [...] Like it's some warning. Some sign for the rest of the mourners to steer fucking clear. [...] Then this old girl there, eighty years old, stood the whole fucking way, she reaches in her bag and she fishes out a can. A fuckin' aerosol. 'Turn round, wean.' And we stand side by side, backs to her and she sprays 'Justice' across both our backs in black fucking aerosol. [...] The whole of the bus puts up this cheer. And they start chanting. 'Justice, justice, justice.'

Pause.

And we ride into Belfast, with the whole bus chanting, singing, all the way into the city.

Swigs again.

By the time we got to St Luke's and the whole place is jammed to standing. They've rigged up speakers but there's four or five helicopters circling the chapel. You can't see or hear a fuckin' thing, just the backs of steaming coats and helicopters. [...] So they bring the coffin out, and that's the first glimpse of the boy from Twinbrook. Six-deep, for nine miles. We crawl our way to the front. And you can see it coming. This black car. With Bobby in the back, draped in the tricolore. And it passes. And as it does, the whole crowd starts chanting your man's name. 'Bobby Sands! Bobby Sands!' The hearse stops outside the gates of the cemetery. And they lift your man out, lift out the coffin and place it on tressels. There's wreaths, Hail Marys, Joyful Mysteries. A piper playing the 'Long Kesh' anthem. Then from the crowd come these four RA, in masks and berets, and draw their pistols and – (*Makes a gunshot sound three times.*) over the coffin. At the graveside, they've got a bullhorn, and you can hear 'em clean over the helicopters. And he quoted Bobby... They used Bobby's own words. [...] 'They have nothing in their whole imperial arsenal... They have nothing in their whole'... ah, how the fuck does it go? ”

The Ferryman

Jez Butterworth

TEN THINGS YOU NEED TO KNOW ABOUT SHANE:

- The year is 1981.
- Shane is seventeen.
- He comes from Derry in Northern Ireland.
- He is a Roman Catholic.
- He lives with his parents and his two younger brothers, Diarmaid and Declan.
- He earns money doing a paper round.
- He likes the music of the time such as punk band The Undertones.
- As we learn in the monologue that follows he has been groomed by the IRA (or Irish Republican Army).
- He has so far only worked as an informer, but has been witness to some of their more violent activities.
- Shane is trusting, honest and sometimes blindly loyal. He is not tough enough to be a natural-born killer. Read the whole play to see where his honesty leads him.

FIVE THINGS TO HELP YOU PERFORM THE MONOLOGUE:

- Firstly you will need to familiarise yourself with Northern Irish politics of the late 1970s and early '80s – 'The Troubles' – and in particular with the imprisoned members of the Irish Republican Army who went on hunger strike to further their cause. 'Bobby's funeral' was the funeral of Bobby Sands, who, for sixty-six days, went on hunger strike before dying at the age of twenty-seven.
- The speech is made up of a conversation that Shane and his two brothers (the Corcoran boys) are having with their

country cousins, the Carney boys. In many ways, the Carney boys have been sheltered from the bitter and dirty feud between the Catholics and Protestants in Northern Ireland, and the Corcoran boys are enjoying showing off. See if you can picture their reactions as you tell the story.

- The boys, who have spent the day bringing in the harvest, have been drinking whiskey, and although Shane should not be discussing IRA business and could be severely punished for doing so, he has been egged on by his brother and he cannot help himself. Have you ever bragged about something despite your better judgement? Without overplaying it you can reference the fact that Shane is drunk, which is why his tongue is loose. You might like to try the speech whilst taking swigs from a bottle (see note on 'using props' in the introduction) – and as obvious as it may sound don't forget to wear a watch!
- The monologue is rich in visual detail and takes in a number of different people and locations. Use your imagination to picture all that he describes.
- It is important that you get the right rhythm and pace in order to create dramatic tension and a good build up to the story. Bear in mind that Shane is enjoying entertaining the boys, and he is good at it. Earlier in the scene, his brother Diarmaid tells them about Bobby Sands' funeral, but Diarmaid hasn't got Shane's 'gift of the gab' and the story falls flat.

Shane

“ Three, four weeks after the funeral, I'm back in town and I'm doing my paper round, going door to door, on the front page there's the news. McCreesh and O'Hara have both starved to death on the same morning. The third and fourth to perish. So I'm delivering the papers when your wee fella rides up on his Grifter there, spotty little cunt about nine years old, and he stops and he asks me if I'm Shane Cocoran. I tell him to do one. But, 'Are you Shane Corcoran? Pat Corcoran's boy?' 'Who wants to know?' 'Mr Muldoon.' […] He says Mr Muldoon wants to talk to you. […] So your wee man on the Grifter says go down McCartney's Café, nine o'clock Saturday morning. And he burns off. So Saturday comes, I go down McCartney's, and I sit down, cup of tea, eyes on the clock. Nine sharp, your man walks in. […] He sits down opposite and he looks at me and he says, 'Are you Shane Corcoran?' And I said yes. (*Beat.*) He starts asking me questions. […] About the paper round. What days. Which streets. He says there's a laundry van, Malone's Laundry. All he wants me to do is make a mental note of when I see it. Make a note of the time and where it stops. I say I haven't got a watch. And he looks at me and he says, 'I saw you there at the funeral last week. Over there in Milltown. Among the crowd.' […] 'I saw you there. At Bobby's funeral.' 'Yes, Mr Muldoon.' 'You boys had something written on your backs there. What was that now?'

Pause.

'Justice.'

Pause.

'And do you want justice, Shane?'

Pause.

'Yes, Mr Muldoon. I want justice. For Bobby.

For Patsy. For us all.' And he goes to his wrist here, and he takes off his watch and he hands it to me. He says, 'Now you've got a watch.' […] So for the next few weeks I'm doing my round, and I see the laundry van there. Malone's Laundry. And I note the time, and where it goes. And each Friday your keed on his Grifter comes by, and I tell him. I don't write nothing down. I just remember. Four weeks ago I'm doing my rounds and I see it there on the front page. Malone's Laundry van blown sky-fucking-high in the Bishops Road. (*Beat.*) They put a parcel under it. Behind the courthouse there. Twenty pounds of Semtex. Guess what? They weren't laundrymen. It's a fucking meat wagon. RUC Black Ops.

Every time they went past there's three of them crouched down in the back there taking pictures of the comings and goings. [...] Not any more. Now all three are in bits all over the Bishops Road. In nine bin bags. ”

The Flick

Annie Baker

TEN THINGS YOU NEED TO KNOW ABOUT AVERY:

- Avery is an African American. Strictly speaking he is twenty, but nineteen will pass, and out of context the monologue can be performed by an actor of any ethnicity.
- He is in love with the movies, and is a film snob.
- He is honest, punctual and organised. He could be described as being obsessive-compulsive.
- A year and a half ago his parents split up.
- Six months after that, Avery tried to commit suicide.
- He has dropped out of college and is living at home with his father, who is a college lecturer.
- He has found a job in a cinema, where the whole play takes place, until he returns to his studies.
- Avery is shy and is sexually awkward.
- He is highly sensitive (particularly to the sight and smell of other people's poo), and he suffers from depression.
- The monologue is a telephone conversation he is having with his therapist.

FIVE THINGS TO HELP YOU PERFORM THE MONOLOGUE:

- Although in the play the therapist is on the telephone, you might like to perform the monologue as if you were in the therapist's consulting room. You could imagine that he/she is sitting down facing you, listening quietly. A therapist will rarely speak or offer advice. Notice how many times Avery says 'Yeah' as if he is trying to fill the silences.
- It is common practice for an analyst or therapist to ask you about your dreams. At last, Avery can remember one. Perhaps Avery is happy that he can finally offer something that might be useful. Perform the monologue with enthusiasm.

- You will need to do some research into the films he names and their directors. Look them up online, and see if you can get a feel for what sort of style they are and what they are about.
- To make the character more personal to you, you may like to substitute Avery's films with films of your own choosing. In which case have a good think about the difference between the 'art-house' movies and the really trashy one. As an example, I loved the film *The Lives of Others*, but I secretly enjoyed *The Man Who Knew Too Little*!
- The significance of the dream. It would seem that Avery is aware that his snobbishness around film is questionable. The things that make you truly happy in life may not be the most outwardly prized or valued but those that touch and speak to you more simply. It's a bit like preferring a bag of chips to a posh dinner.

Avery

“ Oh!

I finally remembered one of my dreams.

Pause.

Yeah.

(*Smiling.*) I *thought* you'd be happy about that. [...]

Okay. So in the dream I'm dead. I mean, I've just died. And I'm in this weird room. Which is basically like purgatory. And there's a whole bunch of us, a bunch of people who just died, and we're all waiting to see if we can, you know, move on. To the next level. Oh. And my dad is there. Because he just died too. And then the room suddenly turns into my dad's study. And this person starts scanning all the books on my dad's bookshelves with this ISBN-type scanner thing and they run the scanner over all of his books and eventually one of the books goes like BEEP BEEP BEEP and the scanner recognizes it and that means my dad is going on to heaven.

And then it's my turn. [...] I'm up next. And suddenly I'm surrounded by all these shelves and on every shelf is every movie I've ever seen. And like some are like DVDs and other are like old VHS tapes from like the nineties and some are even like old thirty-five-millimeter reels, like movies I saw in the theater. And like – yeah. Everything is there. Like The Wizard of Oz, which is the first movie I ever saw. And like old Jim Carrey movies and the entire Criterion Collection... and then they hand me the ISBN scanner and I realize, like, I realize that the way they decide whether or not you get into heaven is through, like, looking at all the movies you've ever watched or all the books you've ever read and figuring out whether there was one book or movie that you truly truly loved. Like one movie that like symbolizes your entire life.

And I think, okay, I'm gonna be fine. I love movies and I've seen all these like awesome movies, this is gonna be no problem, and I start running the scanner across the shelves. I run it across all these Yakuza movies I watched in high school, I run it across all the Truffaut movies, and the scanner isn't beeping. It's weird. It's not recognizing anything. And then I run it over Pierrot le Fou and Barry Lyndon, and I've seen those movies like literally dozens of times, and it doesn't beep. And we're going past hundreds of movies. Really good movies. Movies I like really really love. And I start getting nervous. There's only a couple shelves to go. And I run the scanner over Andrei Rublev and nothing happens. And then I run it over Fanny and Alexander and I can't believe it, but... nothing happens.

And then I think to myself: I'm going to hell.

I haven't truly like, loved or whatever in the right way, I thought I did, but I didn't, and I'm going to hell. And then I'm on the last shelf of movies and I've already like completely lost hope at this point but then suddenly the scanner starts beeping and beeping and I look at the movie that made it beep and it's this like old cruddy VHS tape of Honeymoon in Vegas.

Pause.

Honeymoon in Vegas?

Pause.

It's like this terrible movie with Nicolas Cage and Sarah Jessica Parker from like 1989. I was obsessed with it when I was like four. I watched it at my cousin's birthday party.

It's like a really really bad movie.

Pause.

And at first I'm like: what? My entire life can be represented by Honeymoon in Vegas? Honeymoon in Vegas is like the one movie I truly truly loved? But then I'm like, wait, it doesn't matter, I'm going to heaven. I must have done something right in my life because I'm going to heaven.

And that feeling of like… of like knowing that I made the right choices, was like the best feeling I've ever had.

Yeah.

Pause.

Yeah. […]

Well, yesterday I had this thought.

I was like: okay.

Maybe it's never gonna get better.

Maybe I'm gonna live with my dad for the rest of my life and like the *actual* problem is just that I'm waiting for things to change.

Like maybe I'm just gonna be that weird depressed guy and I should just like accept it.

And that'll be the life I get.

And that'll be okay.

Yeah.

He laughs and rubs a few tears out of his eyes.

Yeah. ”

Forever House

Glenn Waldron

TEN THINGS YOU NEED TO KNOW ABOUT RICHARD:

- The year is 1999, and Richard is sixteen/seventeen.
- Richard is gay, but he is not out yet.
- He comes from Plymouth, in Devon.
- He lives with his mum, dad and nine-year-old sister.
- His family are Methodists, and Richard goes to church three times a week.
- Richard is good at photography and art. His ambition is to study art at Goldsmiths College, although his dad wants him to read law.
- He also likes classical music and used to play the piano.
- His favourite meal is ham, egg and chips.
- Richard is a sensitive soul. He is shy and socially awkward, but also curious about the world.
- Richard suffers from asthma and has to use an inhaler. Read the whole play to find out what happens to him.

FIVE THINGS TO HELP YOU PERFORM THE MONOLOGUE:

- Richard is talking to Graham. Graham is forty-five. He is also gay. He befriended Richard after they met at their local library. They have a shared interest in photography and Graham has invited Richard back to his house to talk more about the subject and to show Richard some of his photography books. They are attracted to one another, but the age difference means that they are also quite awkward. See if you can really picture what Graham looks like. Perhaps you too have felt a similar attraction for an older person. You may already know that feeling of being on the one hand flattered by their attention, but shy and embarrassed because you think that you don't know enough.

- Richard has been drinking red wine and he is not used to it. I don't suggest that you play the monologue drunk, but consider that the wine may have loosened your tongue so that you can let all this out without checking yourself.
- See if you can connect to that feeling of living in a place that you've outgrown. Perhaps you too live in a town that depresses you or where you feel the people are provincial in their outlook. If you don't recognise this feeling, perhaps you can relate to the urge to break free from your family – even if you love them.
- Richard is not out. To what extent does this feeling of being trapped somewhere geographically relate to Richard's homosexuality and inner turmoil at not being able to express himself – as if living in Plymouth is a metaphor for being stuck in the closet? Consider also that his family are religious, and Richard is worried about how his father will react when he tells him that he wants to be an artist and not a lawyer. Use this sensation of not being able to be honest with your family to fuel your need and desire to reach out to Graham. Graham offers a safe space, and over time (read the whole play) they will become lovers. It will help you to remember that the year is 1999. The town itself is run down and being openly gay is arguably harder than it is now.
- If you can't do a Plymouth or general Devon accent, you could try playing the speech in another accent as long as it is obvious that you come from a small town and not a big cosmopolitan city. You could leave out the word Plymouth and try replacing it with somewhere else that you know. However, a word of caution! If you are going to use the monologue for an audition, consider that the panel may know the play and will want a good explanation as to why you have transposed the speech.

Richard

“ [Plymouth?] I think – I think it’s shit. [...] Excuse my language but – I really think it is. It’s completely shit. [...] I think it’s crap. There’s nothing, like – nothing ever happens here – nothing interesting or amazing or – or even anything [horrible]. And most of the people are – like, when they walk, they can barely lift their feet off the ground. I mean, they all walk round like they’re kind-of monged-out most of the time. Haven’t you seen that? [...] Well, they do. And it’s so – I mean – this town, it’s so small. It’s, like, *miniscule* – it doesn’t even have a Pizza Express. [...] Because – because I mean, how can you live all your life somewhere that doesn’t have a Pizza Express? Everyone who lives here, they think it’s the centre of the... But it’s so... Because if they bombed it tomorrow, if they put a great big nuclear bomb under, like, Debenhams and it flattened the whole thing then the rest of the world would be very sad and they’d miss it for a few days and everything but would it – I mean, the world would go on, wouldn’t it? It wouldn’t be like the world couldn’t function any more without the people living in this town. There would be no possibility of the world stopping or – or anything really changing. And after a while, all the people in this town and all the things they’d done, they’d just be, like, memories in other people’s heads. And then, the people that had the memories would die and then they’d just be some people in photographs who nobody knows. Does that make sense? [...] I want to go to London. I’m going to go to London. I want to study there. Art. ”

Foxfinder

Dawn King

TEN THINGS YOU NEED TO KNOW ABOUT WILLIAM:

- William is nineteen.
- He lives in England at a time in the near future or the imagined past when the fox is believed by some to be the enemy of mankind. (Read the whole play to understand how and why this has come about.)
- When William was only five he was sent to the Institute where he was trained to become a foxfinder.
- The Institute was a harsh place and William was strictly disciplined. It meant that he grew up lacking the love and warmth of his parents.
- Foxfinders are responsible for determining whether a farm has been contaminated or not. If they decide that a fox is present, they can confiscate the land and send the farmers to work in factories. As such, William is powerful and even dangerous.
- William is very thin. Foxfinders are required to go hungry as a constant reminder of how close the country has come to starvation.
- William is expected to be 'clean in body and mind', but he has strong sexual urges which confuse him.
- In order to prevent himself from having unclean thoughts or desires, William whips himself.
- When you read the whole play and have a good idea of its message, you will realise that William has been brainwashed.
- At the time of the monologue, William is staying on a farm that is under investigation.

FIVE THINGS TO HELP YOU PERFORM THE MONOLOGUE:

- The book he is clutching is like his bible. Although he is not directly reading from it, the monologue feels as though he is quoting from it. See if you can capture that religious-like fervour that drives the speech.
- The speech is highly descriptive. You will need to have very strong images in your mind of all that he describes. Consider the number of different colours that are mentioned and the number of different animals.
- The word 'beast' is used eight times. This links the fox to our ideas of the Devil, and is meant to instill fear.
- Think about the amount of words to do with death and destruction. For example: 'devoured', 'slaughter', 'disembowel', 'killing', 'deadly', etc.
- It is often said that we hate what we fear in ourselves. When William shudders before he says 'Or sexual perverts', consider that he too is afraid that he may have been contaminated. The final paragraph comes as a warning. It is not unlike certain religious practices that preach sex is a sin.

William

“The red fox, Vulpes Vulpes, is as the name suggests, most usually reddish brown, but its colour ranges to silver and black. It has slender paws, a long muzzle, erect, pointed ears and a tail covered in longer hairs, giving the appearance and name 'brush'. The eyes of the beast are a dull yellow-gold with dark, vertically oriented pupils like those of a cat. Usually the size of a large dog, an adult male can grow up to two and a half metres long from nose to tail tip. Novices should be aware that from a distance, a large brown dog can resemble the beast, but their silhouettes are in fact quite different. Study the diagrams and illustrations that follow and submit them to memory to aid you in your identifications.

The fox is an omnivore and will eat almost anything; fruit, carrion, insects, and small- to medium-sized mammals such as mice and rabbits, unwary cats, small dogs, newborn lambs and sickly calves. Many incidences have been recorded of a mother leaving her baby unguarded outside for only a few seconds, returning to find it gone, taken and devoured. The beast's bloodlust far outstrips its appetite and it will slaughter every hen in a henhouse, leaving the headless carcasses behind. A perfectly evolved killing machine, the beast's teeth can grow up to ten centimetres in length, and its claws can disembowel a man. Sly in nature, the beast is active mainly at dusk and during the night, when it can go about its deadly work unseen.

The beast has influence over the weather, and blights farmers' crops with unseasonable rainfall or periods of drought. It can also cause fires (see 'Fox Fire', Chapter Four), and is riddled with parasites and dangerous diseases to which it is immune but which it revels in spreading about the countryside.

The fox has powers to confuse and can send visions to the mentally unstable and disturb the dreams of the weak. Under its influence, the good and hard-working become fat, lazy alcoholics or…

WILLIAM *is disturbed. He takes a minute to collect himself.*

Or sexual perverts.

Some are victims, turned away from their honest labours unwillingly. Others have allowed the beast to sway their minds or welcomed it with open arms. Differentiating between the guilty and the innocent is very difficult and it is better to view all those living on contaminated farms with suspicion.

You, foxfinder, must be clean in body and mind. Always remember that the smallest fault in your character could become a crack into which the beast may insinuate himself, like water awaiting the freeze that will smash the stone apart. ❞

A Grand Day Out*

Michael Dennis

TEN THINGS YOU NEED TO KNOW ABOUT ANDREW:

- Andrew is seventeen.
- He comes from Nottingham.
- He is gay.
- Although he has had some experience of sex with other boys, he is not out to his parents.
- Andrew is shy.
- The playwright tells us that he 'hasn't quite found his "look" yet' and wears a long overcoat.
- He hated his last school, which he describes as like being in prison, and is now much happier at his sixth-form college.
- He is quite arty and interested in theatre and film.
- He eats vegetarian food, although we don't know how strict he is about this.
- The year is 1994, and Andrew has come to London as the age of gay consent is being debated and voted on in Parliament. When the news comes that the age has been reduced from twenty-one to eighteen, but not the hoped-for sixteen, Andrew and the other demonstrators surge towards the House of Commons and then attempt to block the traffic around Trafalgar Square. This is where he meets Marcus.

FIVE THINGS TO HELP YOU PERFORM THE MONOLOGUE:

- Andrew is already pumped up from the events of the night. To what extent has this given him the courage to go home with a complete stranger? See if you can capture that sense of danger and excitement. He is, after all, 'underage'.

* Published in the volume *Queers*

- Coupled with the thrill of being in this situation, there is also a strange kind of comfort from the fact that Marcus is an accountant, has put the heating on and is making toast and jam. It is as if the sex that is about to follow is made safe by these things.
- What does Marcus look like? See if you can get a very strong image of him. Andrew says later that he didn't particularly fancy Marcus, which made the whole thing easier.
- What does his flat look and feel like? Think about how it might smell to Andrew. When we are in new spaces, especially if we are being intimate with someone, we are often struck by these sensations, as if our senses are on high alert.
- The speech is an extract from a longer monologue. Read the whole thing, and take time to research the significance of the Sexual Offences Bill and the subsequent vote. It wasn't until the year 2001 that the age was reduced to sixteen, bringing it in line with heterosexual sex.

NB This play offers several other monologues from which to choose.

Andrew

❝ So I'd missed my train by this point. And this fella – Marcus – I'd been sitting in the road with, said do I want to come back to his. And I thought, 'Well…' But what do you do? I had nowhere to go. So I did. That's his name, Marcus. Well, course it is! Sorry.

He affects a Spanish accent.

Mark-oos!

We went back to his, his flat, and it was – I mean, it was fine. It was a bit… not… It was okay. I think I'd thought… I mean, it's stupid, I know it is, but I think I'd thought… people in London. But London's just a place, isn't it, like any other. But I suppose you think – 'London!'

I don't mean to sound snobby. It's not snobby. I'm not a snob. My mate Sean's proper bourgeois – though he'd have you believe he's working class cos his dad – I don't know, once drained a radiator or something. But I remember his face when I said we had our tea on our laps on a Sunday watching *Bullseye*. So, I'm not… you know, posh. Anyway. Err. He was asking what I did – Marcus – and I told him, said I was a student and he said he worked for the BBC, in Accounts. So that's interesting, isn't it? Kind of. And I'd said, at the start, that I just needed a place to stay until I could get a train home in the morning, and he'd said that was okay. I was giving off the right vibes, I think. So, it was cool. He's a lot older than me. He's thirty, but he was, um – you know. Nice. He made us some toast and, um, put the heat on. So… it was fine. He had this jam that's made without any sugar. And we talked a bit. He said he'd been on a few, uh, marches and things, you know. Not just – gay. Other stuff. Poll tax and… So that was interesting. And we talked about last night. Called them bastards! Put the – what is it? Put the world to rights. And then he said, 'At least it means *you're* legal now' – cos I'm eighteen. I mean, I'm actually seventeen, but I'd told him I was eighteen cos I thought seventeen sounded a bit young.

Stupid, isn't it? And, I think, when he said that, I thought, '*Right*'… you know? But I just kind of laughed it off. So then he said he should go to bed and he went to get some bedding for me, for the sofa. And…

I think he thought I was a virgin. Which I'm not. But, I mean… I'm not *not* a virgin. But, when he came back in the living room, with the bedding, he was starkers. And I thought –

He exhales – 'Blimey!'

[…]

Funny isn't it? Cos if they'd said yes – if they'd made it sixteen… I'd have gone straight home. ”

Holes in the Skin

Robert Holman

TEN THINGS YOU NEED TO KNOW ABOUT LEE:

- Lee is eighteen years old.
- He comes from a disadvantaged background.
- He lives with his mum on a council estate in Stokesley, north Yorkshire. He says that where he lives is a dump.
- Lee's mother has a drink problem and shows little interest in him.
- He has an older brother called Ewan, who is a small-time drug dealer. Ewan is violent and Lee is afraid of him.
- Lee is described as 'quite thin with light-coloured hair, and he has an ear stud'. In the monologue that follows, he has bare feet and is wearing jeans and a baggy T-shirt. Out of context it doesn't matter about his build or hair colour, but you might take inspiration from the ear stud, bare feet, jeans and baggy T-shirt (see note on what to wear in the introduction).
- As we learn in the monologue that follows, Lee was arrested for having pushed a younger boy off a wall, but although he has served time in a young offenders' prison, he is good at heart, quite shy and hates any trouble.
- While he was in prison, Lee became addicted to heroin.
- Lee fancies a fifteen-year-old girl called Kerry who has recently moved to the same street, but Kerry fancies Lee's 'bad boy' brother as much as she fancies Lee.
- The only person who has shown enduring love and support for Lee is an older middle-class woman called Freya. She lives in another village, and although she has a son of her own, she has taken Lee under her wing, made him her project and tries her best to help him. Read the whole play to learn more about their unusual relationship.

FIVE THINGS TO HELP YOU PERFORM THE MONOLOGUE:

- Lee is from north Yorkshire. If the accent is not native to you, you could try performing the speech in an accent that you are familiar with. Make sure you choose something that fits in with his background.
- Lee is talking to Kerry and her mother. They know that Lee has been in prison, and when Kerry asks Lee what it was he did, the monologue that follows is his response. See if you can picture Kerry and her mum. What do they look like? Imagine their reactions. Remember that Lee really fancies Kerry, and so it is important that he gives a good account of himself.
- Think about his need to set the record straight and the different ways he tries to elicit their sympathy. He repeatedly says that it wasn't his fault, for example: 'I didn't mean to do it', 'It was an accident', 'I didn't intend', 'I was a kid', etc. He also chooses to paint a picture of himself as the victim when he says, 'Unfortunately for me', 'I could tell he didn't like us', 'I was already being bullied' and 'I wasn't coping at all well'.
- Lee is addicted to heroin. You don't need to play the speech either high on drugs or coming down from a trip and desperate for the next hit, but be aware of Lee's edginess and overall inability to deal with life.
- Deerbolt is a young offenders' establishment in County Durham. If you change Lee's accent you may prefer to change this reference to a young offenders' institution that is closer to where you are placing him.

Lee

" I didn't mean to do it. I had a fracas with a schoolkid once. [I broke his neck] [...] Unfortunately for me. I suppose more unfortunately for him actually. I pushed him off a wall. It was an accident. He overbalanced. They said I pushed him, but I didn't really. I got four years for it. I was guilty of GBH with intent. I didn't intend. They said I should have foresaw the consequences. I was fifteen. The boy was eleven. A lot was made of that in court with the judge and the jury and everything. That's what swung it against us. Also I looked older by the time I came to court. The lad was in a wheelchair which didn't help us. All the sympathy was bound to be with him. And when my antecedence was read out I'd got shoplifting charges, and cautions and all that. The judge said he'd no choice but to send me down. He said I was on a slippery slope and a very dangerous young man. I wasn't a young man. I was a kid who'd just done something on the spur of the moment for no reason. The only person who cared was Freya. Freya came to court with us every day. They sent me mam away for shouting at the little boy when he was giving his evidence. The judge told the jury they had to disregard her impudence. How could they? He didn't when he sentenced me, after he'd read all the reports. I could tell he didn't like us, he made it very clear. He ignored the psychiatrist who said a long prison sentence wasn't the best option for us. I was already being bullied in Deerbolt, so I know what he meant. It was me who'd told him anyway. I told him I'd been raped by two bully boys in the showers, one after the other, and one who just watched and didn't do it. I told him I wasn't coping at all well. ”

Home

Nadia Fall

TEN THINGS YOU NEED TO KNOW ABOUT GARDEN BOY:

- The play is a piece of verbatim theatre based on interviews, so Garden Boy is a real person.
- Garden Boy is eighteen.
- He is described as 'a young white man, born and bred in East London'.
- Garden Boy is very proud of his cockney roots, but also loves the mix of races and cultures where he lives.
- Garden Boy is proud, determined and motivated. He would like to get a job in a supermarket, and his main goal in life is to look after and provide for his little brother, who is nine.
- Following rows with his mother, Garden Boy left home when he was sixteen and lived rough on the streets.
- Garden Boy now lives in a place called Target East, which is a hostel specifically for the young homeless.
- Garden Boy has only met his father once in his life when he was seventeen. His father lives in Birmingham, and Garden Boy can't afford the fare to see him.
- Garden Boy was bullied at school and struggles with anxiety and depression.
- He is referred to as Garden Boy because one day he would love a home with a garden. He says that having somewhere to be outdoors – a garden or a balcony – would help him to relax.

FIVE THINGS TO HELP YOU PERFORM THE MONOLOGUE:

- Because Garden Boy is a real person, his identity has been protected. Use the opportunity to create a fully rounded character for yourself and start by giving him a name. From what you know of Garden Boy, what do you imagine he could be called?

- The language here is conversational, loose and more like an improvisation than a carefully structured text. Bear in mind that the characters are being interviewed and the script is made up of their responses. See if you can capture that ease of being in the moment, not planning what you will say, but letting thoughts come to you as you go along. It should appear that Garden Boy is just chatting.
- Garden Boy is willing to talk about his life. Perhaps it is a relief for him to be able to share and confide in someone he can trust. See if you can imagine the interviewer, and the room or office in which the interview is taking place, so that you have a focus for the speech. Enjoy being able to offload and see if you can picture the interviewer's reactions.
- Garden Boy has a sensitive personality, and it is important that you convey this. He suffers from anxiety and depression and is scared of the other residents in his block. It will help to consider his upbringing – the fact that he comes from a broken home, is unwanted by his mother, unsupported by his father and was bullied at school.
- Garden Boy has a garden trowel in his hand. You might like to try the monologue holding one (see note on using props in the introduction). Imagine that you have been gardening in the communal courtyard. Do you have a similar hobby that helps you to unwind?

Garden Boy

“I've been here nearly two years… and it's been struggling, struggling living here, it's just hard. Uh, well me and my mum, my mum had my little brother when I was sixteen… and then all my mum did was say, make him a drink, make your brother food, do this, do that, do this, I literally had no time to myself, except for night-time and then obviously I was awake all the way through the night, tired during the day and I had to do more stuff and it led – it led to depression and anxiety… I didn't even go school because I used to basically just had to do so much for my mum, plus I was bullied at school so that didn't help either. Mum didn't care. And then... one day I snapped, and, had a go at my mum and then she wanted me to leave so I left... I was on the streets for about a month... or so, I used to sleep in the park up the road on the benches, then I eventually had the courage to tell my girlfriend? I lived with her for a couple of months... then I went First Point, and then... I ended up here.

A home? A place where I feel safe... walk in, cos like here, I walk in, I literally, put the latch on... the chain, and the bottom lock... and then I put a towel at the bottom?... and I think that's quite sad that I don't feel safe even though there's security, two electric doors and then my door.

The people that live here to be exact, just, you walk around and you see like, there's a guy called Blunt who I know, lives a few doors away from me, I'm not sure if I should be saying this but...

He's umm he said to me that um, he was caught for burglary and I'm like, okay, this guy lives three doors down from me and he's been done for burglary, there's drug dealers in the building... there's people who grow drugs, and there's just, it just doesn't feel like a safe environment, cos when I first moved in here, I think it was about two months after moving in here some guy got stabbed in the neck.

In this, in the building yeah.

I don't know if fatally, I know he got stabbed in the neck.

I feel more safer out there than I do in here. ”

Home

Nadia Fall

TEN THINGS YOU NEED TO KNOW ABOUT SINGING BOY:

- The play is a piece of verbatim theatre based on interviews, so Singing Boy is a real person.
- Singing Boy is seventeen.
- He is from south London.
- He comes from a disadvantaged background.
- He is described as 'slight' and 'mixed-race'. However, out of context he could look like you.
- He thinks he might be gay, but he hasn't come out yet.
- Singing Boy has been rejected by his mother and his mother's boyfriend, and they have kicked him out of his home.
- Singing Boy is now living in a place called Target East, which is a hostel specifically for the young homeless.
- Since leaving his mother's house he is much happier. He has left his old school where he was bullied and is now at a college where he can concentrate on the performing arts.
- Singing Boy is sensitive and caring. He likes cooking and is a natural home-maker. Read the whole play to see what happens to him.

FIVE THINGS TO HELP YOU PERFORM THE MONOLOGUE:

- Because Singing Boy is a real person, his identity has been protected. Use the opportunity to create a fully rounded character for yourself and start by giving him a name. From what you know of Singing Boy, what do you imagine he could be called?
- The language here is conversational, loose and more like an improvisation than a carefully structured text. Bear in mind

that the characters are being interviewed and the script is made up of their responses. See if you can capture that ease of being in the moment, not planning what you will say but letting thoughts come to you as you go along. It should appear that Singing Boy is just chatting.

- Singing Boy is really happy to talk about his life. Perhaps it is a relief for him to be able to share and confide in someone he can trust. See if you can imagine the interviewer, and the room or office in which the interview is taking place, so that you have a focus for the speech. Enjoy being able to offload and see if you can picture the interviewer's reactions.
- There is a contrast in the monologue between the past and the present. It could be that in Singing Boy's mind the past is a dark place and the present (and future) a bright one. Perhaps you can connect to that feeling of things improving in your life, of feeling free when you have previously felt trapped. It is important that you capture the sense of hope in Singing Boy's story and the determination he feels to make a better life for himself.
- Think about how you will depict his sensitivity. He keeps himself to himself and steers away from trouble. He is questioning his sexuality. Without overplaying this characteristic, work to find a gentleness about him that sets him apart.

Singing Boy

" My mum's house really… No, I consider my place as a home as well, here as well… but still feel a bit… maybe because I'm NEW I still feel a bit… you know I don't, I still feel, I don't feel this is my home YET. But as the months go by and start getting my things together, I can call it more of a home.

Well – (*Pause.*) well – (*Smiling.*) what led me to living at Target is basically I got kicked out of home when I was seventeen I didn't want to go back. So they put me in a hostel and then from there step by step, eventually step by step… I was sent here, they 'referred' me here.

Um, no. Because I'm very to m… I keep myself to myself. Because there are a lot of people in this building and you don't even want to mess about with… There's people in this building that do drugs and all sorts. I'm a person who wants to keep WELL, well away from that. I keep my head down, because I don't want anyone to think I'm either giving them a dirty look or what I've seen in this building is that people get very – (*Clicks fingers.*) aggravated so I want to avoid that and that's why I always mind my own business.

I've had problems with my mum for quite a while. And not just because of my mum, I mean Mum played parts obviously, but I'm not saying here that I was an angel because obviously I'm not… her boyfriend as well was getting involved but even before that, even before he came into the picture, there was already issues between us. But then that added on the tension, you know building up, and that made it so… whatever. But I remember the exact day that I left: it was the eighth of January at seven p.m. What I left, well I didn't leave, I got kicked out, and the police got involved but the police told me that, 'if your mum wants you to leave have to leave, then you have to leave'. But what they did not know, well they knew my age, but obviously they were ignorant to the fact, that even though I'm seventeen… she can't ask me to leave by law you still have to be with your mum.

Well my mum used to hit me before but not now. But shouting, swearing at me obviously.

And there was even a point my mum said to me, she said to me, 'I wish I aborted you.' (*Pause.*)

And from that day on I said Okay – (*Pause.*) I'm going to stop trying to give a damn, I'm going to stop, trying to every time do things for people. Because I'm going to just do me.

What now? My days I wake up in the morning, I feel absolutely great. I get to do what I want, every moment I go to college. I sing I get do this it's part of my course. I sing, I dance, I act… I do everything. You want me to sing something now? Do you know Beyoncé? Yeah I'll sing that.

He sings 'Halo' by Beyoncé.

Thanks. Well what keeps me very motivated is the fact that every song I pick, every song I sing has to have meaning behind it and I feel that with every song I sing I'm here for a purpose, I'm here for a reason, to show the world… I was born. When I was at school, a all-boys school. I went to an all-boys school and it was not the easiest thing to get up on that stage and sing and not have people laugh at you. Or after you've finished your performance to say you're gay because you're singing or you're gay because you're singing a female song… And plus the way my voice sounds I felt every day I walked through those gates, I could have died.

The first time I fell in love, you can ask me that.

Silence.

I will tell you now… One thing, the only thing that I missed is that I have this one issue now in my sexuality… right now I don't know… where I'm going. I'm not sure what I like. I haven't told my family and I'm not planning to right now. Not at the moment I don't think… but that's one thing actually to tell you, I don't know. I'm…

I'm still struggling with that. But eventually I'll get to the bottom of it and hopefully soon.

My key workers the people who advise me, they're nice guys, if you stay here peacefully, keep your head down, like no warnings – nothing – you'll get your place one day – not straight away obviously but eventually. I respect everyone, I obey the rules, I do everything like – stay strong. ❞

Home

Nadia Fall

TEN THINGS YOU NEED TO KNOW ABOUT TATTOO BOY:

- The play is a piece of verbatim theatre based on interviews, so Tattoo Boy is a real person.
- Tattoo Boy is about eighteen or nineteen.
- He is from east London.
- He comes from a disadvantaged background.
- He is described as 'a young white man with many tattoos on his arms and neck'. Out of context he doesn't have to have tattoos, but he should be played by a white actor.
- Tattoo Boy is proud of his English heritage and has a problem with the number of people from other countries who are living in London. It's important to remember that his views are not those of the writer.
- Tattoo Boy didn't see much of his mother when he was younger and was largely brought up by his sister.
- Even before secondary school, Tattoo Boy was getting into trouble, stealing sweets and alcohol from nearby factories.
- Tattoo Boy is now living in a place called Target East, which is a hostel specifically for the young homeless.
- He has a Turkish girlfriend and enjoys hanging out with his friends and smoking weed. A year ago, a good friend of his was murdered in a shopping mall.

FIVE THINGS TO HELP YOU PERFORM THE MONOLOGUE:

- Because Tattoo Boy is a real person, his identity has been protected. Use the opportunity to create a fully rounded character for yourself and start by giving him a name. From what you know of Tattoo Boy, what do you imagine he could be called?

- The language here is conversational, loose and more like an improvisation than a carefully structured text. Bear in mind that the characters are being interviewed and the script is made up of their responses. See if you can capture that ease of being in the moment, not planning what you will say but letting thoughts come to you as you go along. It should appear that Tattoo Boy is just chatting.
- Tattoo Boy is willing to talk about his life. Perhaps it is a relief for him to be able to share and confide in someone he can trust. See if you can imagine the interviewer, and the room or office in which the interview is taking place, so that you have a focus for the speech. Enjoy being able to offload and see if you can picture the interviewer's reactions.
- Tattoo Boy's has some offensive views; however, it is important that you don't stereotype him or demonise him in any way. He may be uneducated, but he is also honest, and it is important to go beyond his apparent ignorance to try to understand why he is so fearful in the first place. Although the play was written before the vote to leave the European Union, it acts as a kind of indication of what could happen if white working-class views are ignored by those in power.
- Tattoo Boy has anger-management problems. Later on in the play he smashes a light bulb. What is interesting is just how articulate he is about how his upbringing has contributed to his feelings of hurt and neglect. He is aware that he has lacked his mother's love, and although he can't always control his rage, he is regretful of his past mistakes. See if you can fuse his specific feeling of having been ignored by his mother with his more general feelings of being overlooked by society.

Tattoo Boy

“Round this area, I ain’t racist or anything but this is mainly like, a black person’s area, where I’m white and I don’t dress with all the fucking tracksuits and trousers past my asshole and that, I don’t get pulled over d’you know what I mean? Yeah. Cos the black people stereotype theirself anyway, so, they’ve only got theirself to blame. They say ‘we’re the minority’, but did you read on the news yesterday, the majority are now the minority.

In London, all together, white people are the minority. White, English people are minority.

Africans are the majority and then Caribbeans then Asians.

Because you see um… Polish shops, Jamaican shops, dadadada, but then if you see like an English shop or something, someone will blatantly come out with ‘oh that’s racist’. You know that you know how it works cos for instance you go to Poland, you go to China, you go to India… you’ll never see a, a church of England there or anything, you’ll never see a shop saying, ‘oh, only English shop’ and that, I’m not saying that only English people or Polish shops that are here only Polish people are allowed in them but they don’t have just like, an English shop will have food for every other country that’s why you don’t even really need to leave London to travel the world and that, you see it all, it’s multicultural, but, the problem is, it’s out of control now d’you know what I mean like you…

Nowadays, you have to keep your own… you have to keep the history of the country going d’you know what I mean? Within a hundred years’ time this country won’t even have history d’you know what I mean if you think from all over the world it’ll be there won’t be one English person, I don’t reckon, in about a hundred years. They’ll all have some other different ethnic minority or background. Like you know I’m saying, no matter, everyone who’s come to this country, yeah, like all different foreign people you go back to any one of them foreign countries and I guarantee you they still have their native people there sort of thing you know what I mean?

My girlfriend's not English, she's Turkish. Doesn't bother me. (*Pause.*) Doesn't bother me at all but I'm just saying enough's enough like because for instance, if you go to them other countries you won't see none of our shit in their country and even in, even though this is England you'll never see English stuff in this country d'you understand what I'm saying. Like I went Wilkinson the other day and the only flags they sell are Pakistani and Nigeria. In the English shop, Wilkinson and where the fuck is the English flag then… oh yeah and Polish flag they sold, I'm like, just because they're white don't mean they're English d'you know what I mean, they're fucking Polish man.

And like everyone who's not English like, they're just rinsing the country, bleeding it dry and when someone English just tries bleeding the country dry cos they're actually suffering because all these foreigners are bleeding their country dry, they get in trouble and they get fucked right up. […] England just gets the piss taken out of it d'you know what I mean? That's all it is it's a piss-takers' country. Bunch of mugs like. ”

Jonesy*

Tom Wells

TEN THINGS YOU NEED TO KNOW ABOUT JAMIE:

- Jamie is fifteen and from a small town.
- He loves GCSE PE, but he suffers from asthma.
- He also loves books, drizzle and Hobnobs.
- He is very close to his mum, and he loves dancing to Jessie J in his bedroom.
- He is funny and sensitive.
- Because of this, people often make fun of him.
- His nickname is 'Jonesy', because his last name is Jones and his PE teacher likes to put a 'y' after people's surnames.
- Jamie likes this, it makes him feel like he belongs, like he fits in.
- Although he feels like the underdog, Jamie is a fighter. He is determined not to let his ill-health get the better of him.
- In order to pass the PE exam you have to choose two sports. Jamie already plays football, but after suffering an asthma attack during a rugby match, Jamie decides to join the girls' class and take netball.

FIVE THINGS TO HELP YOU PERFORM THE MONOLOGUE:

- The monologue comes at the very start of the play. Jamie is introducing himself to us. You will need to talk directly to the audience (see note on talking to the audience in the introduction).
- The rugby incident, in which he nearly dies, is the start of his story. It is the reason he takes up netball, which is far less dangerous. Read the whole play to see what happens next and why this introduction is so important.

* Published in the volume *Jumpers for Goalposts* by Tom Wells

- Think about Jamie's physicality. Do you have asthma or know anyone with asthma? How does it affect you/them? What is it/might it be like to have to carry an inhaler with you at all times?
- Jamie is funny. Despite the fact that he is unwell, he has a great sense of humour and is very good at poking fun at himself. When it gets to the bit where his 'theme tune swells' and he falls over, see if you can hum something that could underscore this moment, like in a film. You could also have fun with the way he drops to the ground and has his asthma attack. Of course, in real life this would be serious and potentially frightening, but here Jamie wants to entertain us and make light of his condition.
- To what extent does his survival at school rely on this 'class clown' behaviour? Is it a way of trying to be popular and/or coping with feelings of being the odd one out? You decide.

Jamie

“ Jamie Jones.
'Jonesy.'
Fifteen years of age.
If I had to describe myself I'd say, oh I dunno I'd say:
Just a small-town boy.
With asthma.

JAMIE *shows us his inhaler.*

I love: books. I love drizzle. Hobnobs.
Love my mum. I love dancing round my bedroom in my pants to this:

'Price Tag' by Jessie J.

I really love GCSE PE.
They said it couldn't be done. Cos of my breathing and so on.
They said

'Do geography instead, Jamie. You love plate tectonics.'

But I said 'no.' Said I'd prove them wrong.
Because more than anything, more than anything in this world, I love: films where the underdog unexpectedly triumphs over adversity to achieve his or her dreams. Ideally through the medium of sport. [...]
And now, my own life.

The true real-life story of Jamie 'Jonesy' Jones: Underdog. Potentially.
I'm not sure how it ends yet.

I'm not sure if I get to achieve my dream of passing GCSE PE against the odds.
Might just be a div in skimpy shorts.

First things first: becoming an underdog.
It's dead easy actually.
It just happens.
For me, it happens like this.
I'm face down in the mud.
The mud is going in my mouth and in my gum shield.
It is the first time I've ever worn a gum shield in my whole entire life.
I'm buried under approximately fifteen burly rugby players.
I'm buried under fifteen burly rugby players and I'm doing two things:
One. I'm imagining what my theme tune would sound like if I had a theme tune.
It's pretty stirring.
– Two. I'm having a massive asthma attack.
Together it sounds like this.

JAMIE*'s theme tune swells.*
He drops to the floor and has an asthma attack for a bit.
His theme tune stops.
He stands up.

In the ambulance.
Heading to the hospital.
The lights are flashing but the siren's not on. [...]
Lauren, the paramedic, is giving me oxygen, tons of it.

It's nice actually.
When she saw it was me slowly choking to death on the rugby pitch she just rolled her eyes and went

'You again.'

I gave her a big thumbs-up in a 'what-am-I-like?' sort of a way.
I think it's called 'having a rapport'.
So it's good.
I mean it's not ideal but.
I am probably going to fail my GCSE PE now, given that Mr Small went mad because I'm not technically meant to play contact sports and I hadn't said.
I just wanted to see what would happen.
I wasn't expecting a near-death experience.
Deano goes

'I'll come see you after school. Text me what ward you're on. I'll bring sweets.'

So. Plenty to look forward to.
For now though, I'm just gasping into the oxygen mask, pondering how I got into this pickle.
We normally do football, me and Deano.
I love it, I love playing football.
I enjoy the sport, I enjoy the camaraderie, I enjoy the skimpy shorts.
It is also how I got my nickname
'Jonesy'. ❞

Jumpers for Goalposts

Tom Wells

TEN THINGS YOU NEED TO KNOW ABOUT LUKE:

- Luke is nineteen.
- He comes from Hull in the north-east of England. If you are not from Hull, you can play the speech in your own accent.
- He is gay.
- He is socially awkward and shy.
- He works as a librarian.
- It was in the library where he met Danny.
- Danny put up a poster for an amateur football team called Barely Athletic and convinced him to come and play.
- Danny is HIV positive, but did not tell Luke straight away.
- They started a relationship and stole their first kiss in the football changing room.
- When Luke found out that Danny had AIDS, he panicked and broke up with him.

FIVE THINGS TO HELP YOU PERFORM THE MONOLOGUE:

- Luke is talking to Danny. He last saw Danny two weeks ago when Danny told him that he was HIV positive. Since then Luke has had time to process the fact, and he is now okay with it. This new thinking needs to underpin the speech and is the reason that Luke has come back. Perhaps you too have received news that was initially shocking and took some time to get over.
- The monologue has a real sense of urgency. You will need to feel that this is the last chance you will get to explain yourself and to win Danny back. In other words, the stakes are high and you must not pre-empt the successful outcome.

- The diary excerpts are Luke's trump card. Deliver this second part of the monologue as though you are offering Danny a glimpse of the real you. Danny brought the poster into the library because he fancied Luke, and he would have had no idea that Luke had felt the same. Luke is hoping that this revelation will be enough to secure/rekindle their relationship.
- Although Luke is serious, the monologue is very funny. See if you can capture that quirky way Luke has of speaking. He fusses over small details, is nervy and probably isn't even aware that he is being funny.
- Think about how you will play the final lines about the condom. Here Luke *is* being brave. However, he is also typically practical in his choice of 'ribbed, extra-safe', because he doesn't want to get infected. See if you can contrast this with the flirtatious afterthought of 'pineapple' and 'exotic'. Perhaps he is aware that he might have ruined the moment with his concerns about safety, hoping to regain some ground with the more sensual mention of fruit.

Luke

“ Danny, please. [...] I know I fucked up, Danny. I know I did. You said it and I just, I panicked – [...]

But then, as soon as I was the other side of the door, honestly, I was just like: Luke, you absolute idiot. Don't leave him. Get back in there. Hug him. But I was scared I'd get it wrong, say the wrong thing cos, I didn't know what to say. So I didn't. But I wish I had done. I really wish I had done so. Just thought, today, just wanted to check really. Just – and it's fine to say no but, just in case: wondered if we could maybe sort of, yeah, have another go? Cos, yeah. I'd love that to be honest.

Don't say no yet, not yet, just. One second cos... There's some stuff I should've, ages ago but. I just, I didn't so... Um. Yeah.

LUKE *looks in his diary. Finds the page.*

'Porridge boiled over in the microwave this morning. It is actually quite a tricky stain to clean so I missed the 77. Got the 75 instead. It goes via Burstwick and Holderness Road. Got in late.' [...]

Just, just bear with me. Please.

'Spent two hours trying to re-shelve Mills and Boons without disturbing a sleeping tramp. Jacket potato for lunch.

That lad came in again this afternoon. Brought a poster.

And I wanted to just. I dunno.

He is the most beautiful thing I've ever seen in Adidas trackies. When he's there I just want to shout my life is boring please be in it. Across the library. Just shout. I nearly did today but then I thought it could go either way so I just breathed really hard instead. Probably sounds daft but he smells immense and now there's little particles of him up my nose. Which is a bit like having sex maybe. I dunno.

You know when you fancy someone so much you could just vom? Just throw up your whole life in front of him like: have it. Please. Let's go on adventures, you can meet my nan. It's like that. But also a bit like having a stroke. In a good way. Heart and head and, you know. Limbs. And when he leaves you're just like: numb.

I want to wear his jumpers. Doubt they'd fit but.

Wish I was braver. Wish I was better at football.'

LUKE *stops reading.*

Honestly, Danny, there's no one in the world I'd rather put a condom on than you.

LUKE *fishes in his pocket.*

Got ribbed, extra-safe. Pineapple. [...]

Thought: exotic. ”

Kes

Lawrence Till
Adapted from Barry Hines' novel A Kestrel for a Knave

TEN THINGS YOU NEED TO KNOW ABOUT BILLY:

- The story takes place in the late 1960s/early '70s, and Billy is fifteen.
- He comes from a mining village near Barnsley in south Yorkshire.
- He comes from a poor, working-class background, and when he leaves school he is expected to go down the pit (i.e. become a miner).
- He lives on a rough estate with his mother and older brother Jud. Neither his mother nor brother are kind to Billy. They make him do most of the chores, and the money that Billy gets from doing a paper round goes straight back to his mum.
- Billy's father left his mother when Billy was only six years old. Since then Billy's mother has had a string of boyfriends.
- Billy often goes hungry, and steals chocolate from the shop and juice and eggs from the milkman.
- Billy struggles with school work. He barely reads and is useless at sport.
- Billy is constantly picked on by the teachers, who hit him with a cane, and by the other schoolchildren, who poke fun and pick fights with him. He says of himself, 'I seem to get into bother for nowt'.
- Billy is a dreamer. He loves comics and enjoys acting out the stories from *The Dandy*.
- Billy has found a kestral in the woods. He keeps it in a shed and has taught himself to train it.

FIVE THINGS TO HELP YOU PERFORM THE MONOLOGUE:

- Billy's accent and way of speaking is very important. As you will see from the way it is written the Yorkshire dialect is part of the text. For example words like 't' to mean 'the', 'owt' meaning 'anything', and 'nowt' meaning 'nothing' tell you how it should be spoken. I would not advise performing this speech in any other accent. The book and film are so well known that it will seem odd and even wrong to transpose it. You may like to read the book and watch the film *Kes* directed by Ken Loach. However, be careful that you don't just copy Dai Bradley's performance – see if you can find your own interpretation.

- Billy adores his kestrel, or 'Kes' as he has named her. She is the only good thing in his life and compensates for the unhappiness he feels at home and at school. With Kes he can be free. He can experience love – both *for* the bird and *from* the bird. It is an unfamiliar sensation for Billy and crucial that, when you play the speech, you can convey his sense of wonder and excitement at the strong connection that they have. Before this monologue starts he says, 'I feel as though she is doing me a favour, just letting me be her friend.'

- Billy has taught himself how to train Kes from a book on falconry that he stole from the library. The 'creance' is a fine line used to leash the hawk during training. The 'jess' is a leather strap attached to the leg of the bird in order for the trainer to tether and control the bird when it is resting on the glove. It would be a good idea to read up on all of this so that you can get a better idea of how it all works. It will help you to visualise all that Billy describes.

- Billy is talking to his teacher Mr Farthing. Mr Farthing is kind and shows a genuine interest in Billy. It is the lunch hour, and Mr Farthing has come to the field where Billy keeps Kes. See if you can imagine what Mr Farthing looks like. Perhaps you can base him on a teacher at your own school. Also imagine the field, the sense of being outdoors. You will also need to picture the kestrel herself.

- Billy is underprivileged and is constantly being told that he will amount to nothing. However, discovering this rare talent for training birds has given Billy a reason to get up in the morning. It is has given him a sense of pride and a genuine hope for the future. On a wider level, *Kes* represents the possibilities for all marginalised or disaffected young people. Of course, you can't play that idea, but you must connect to that feeling of being excellent at something when all else fails. You could equate Billy's talent for falconry with your own desire to act or to be involved in drama. They are similar gifts because they are rare, instinctive and cannot necessarily be taught.

NB This play offers other monologues for the other teenage characters.

Billy

“The most exciting time was when I let her fly free for t' first time. I'd been flying Kes on t' creance for about a week, and she was coming to me owt up to thirty, forty yards, and it says in t' books that when it's coming this far, straight away, it's ready to fly loose. I daren't though, sir. I kept saying to myself, I'll just use t' creance today to make sure, then I'll fly her free tomorrow. But when tomorrow came I did the same thing again. Tomorrow. Tomorrow. I did this for about a week than I got right mad with myself 'cos I knew I'd have to do it some day. So on t' last night I didn't feed her up, just to make sure that she'd be sharp set next morning. I hardly went to sleep that night, I was thinking about it that much.

I wake up and I think right, if she flies off, she flies off, and it can't be helped. I go down to t' shed. She's dead keen an all, walking about on her shelf behind t' bars, and screaming out when she sees me coming. I take her out in t' field and try her on creance first time, and she comes first time, an' she comes like a rocket. I think, right this time.

I unclip creance, take swivel off an let her hop on to t' fence post. There is nowt stopping her now. She just stands there with her jesses on. She can take off and there is nowt I can do about it. I am terrified. I think, she's forced to go, she's forced to, she'll just fly off and that'll be it. But she doesn't. She just sits there looking around while I back off into t' field. I go right into t' middle, then hold my glove up and shout her.

Come on Kes! Come on then!

Nowt happened at first. Then, just as I go walk back to her, she comes. You ought to have seen her. Straight as a die, about a yard off t' floor. And t' speed! She comes twice as fast as when she had creance on, 'cos it used to drag in t' grass and slow her down. She comes like lightning, head dead still, and her wings never make a sound, then wham! Straight up onto my glove, claws out grabbing for t' meat. I am that pleased I don't know what to do with myself. Well, that's it. I've done it. I'd trained her. I trained her. ”

Little Baby Jesus

Arinzé Kene

TEN THINGS YOU NEED TO KNOW ABOUT KEHINDE:

- Kehinde is sixteen.
- He is black.
- He lives in a rough, inner-city part of London.
- He is described as 'mature, very sensible for his age, but there is a sensitivity about him; an innocence'.
- He has an older brother and a twin sister called Taiwo to whom he is devoted. Read the play to find out what happens to her.
- Kehinde describes himself as having 'mixed-race-girl' syndrome. He says he over-fancies girls with a lighter skin than him. At one point in his life he even wished and prayed that he could be mixed-race too.
- His first mixed-race girlfriend was called Rachel, but he wasn't really in love with her. Later on in the play he will develop feelings for a mixed-race girl called Joanne.
- He is not comfortable around white grown-up men, which might explain why he is so understanding of his grandmother in the monologue that follows.
- At his school there is a gang of white boys. Although Kehinde knows it is wrong, he tries to cosy up to them because he is afraid of what they might do to him.
- Kehinde comes from a religious background. He believes in God and, according to his faith, comes to realise that while God can sometimes be harsh, he is also merciful.

FIVE THINGS TO HELP YOU PERFORM THE MONOLOGUE:

- Read the start of the play before performing this monologue. In a speech that comes before this one, Kehinde has already talked about his grandmother and how she disapproves of his light-skinned girlfriends. It will give a good background to this monologue and set you up.

- See if you can chart the journey from Kehinde finding the situation funny, 'I... didn't wanna miss a sniffle', to realising that his grandmother's behaviour is out of control.
- Be sensitive to the situation. On the one hand you pity the girl, and on the other you understand the politics behind your grandmother's outburst. Kehinde has a keen sense of history and is very good at seeing the complexity beyond a single action.
- Kehinde is intelligent. See if you can capture this thinking quality when performing the monologue, as if you are trying to work things out as you say them.
- You will need to have a very strong 'memory' of the events you describe. Really imagine the scene as if you are playing a short film in your head. What do the other characters look like? Think about the bedroom, the detail of the curtains, the boots sticking out underneath them, etc.

NB This play offers a number of other monologues from which to choose.

Kehinde

“The day my brother brought this white girl back it was as if Grandma just knew, like she had some sixth sense or something. As soon as she come through the door, she puts the shopping bags down on the kitchen table, where I was watching TV. Normally she'd start packing the food into the fridge, I'd automatically stand up to boil the water for the vegetables before she had a chance to tell me how lazy I was, but no, not today. She marched straight up the stairs and made a beeline to my brother's room – didn't even take off her jacket. Most days, she'd just stand in his doorway and ask him why he weren't doing his homework or why he only vacuumed downstairs but today she must've smelt the sex-funk or something. She went all the way into his room. Shut the door behind her. When I heard that door click shut I had to crack a smile though, cos my brother was always getting away with things. I went and sat on the stairs, didn't wanna miss a sniffle.

White girl is hiding, behind the curtains. Grandma notices the pair of UGG boots sticking out from the bottom. My brother is sat at his desk, with his eyes on a page apparently halfway through some novel. Fooling nobody – he doesn't read. Grandma walks straight over to the curtain and punches it. The curtain screams. She punches it a bag of times. A barrage of punches later and the drapes fall down. She spat in the face of a little white girl somewhere between fourteen and sixteen years old and then gave her the beating of her life.

When she was done she sat on the corner of my brother's bed – sweating, breathing heavily. She had folds of pink skin under her fingernail from when she'd scratched the girl's eyelids. She beat that white girl bad. She beat that white girl like she was the white woman who my granddad cheated on her with. She beat that white girl like she was the white bus driver who closed the doors in her face after she ran all that way to catch it. She beat that white girl like she was the white man in the market who gave her ten pounds' change when she remembers giving him the twenty-pound note that she *just* got from the bank. She beat that white girl the way she would've loved to beat the white woman in customs who made her throw away all the food she had in her hand luggage.

Grandma had a heart condition, so when the white police came to arrest her, the white paramedics came too. She felt that white people had taken everything away from her. So as they were putting her in handcuffs and she was calling them devils and Lucifers and demons, obviously they thought she was crazy. But I knew she wasn't crazy. She wasn't crazy she was just hurt. And conditioned. And that's how she'd be until the perishing day because it's hard trying to tell old people new things when they're stuck in 1974.

My uncle came over to our house that evening and you know what he said to me? He said –

'Kehinde, you are her trophy child, you know that? She has looked after you since you had no teeth so you have to look after her until her teeth fall out.'

Family are so shifty. They are always trying to pass on the responsibility. ❞

Little Baby Jesus

Arinzé Kene

TEN THINGS YOU NEED TO KNOW ABOUT RUGRAT:

- Rugrat is fifteen/sixteen.
- He is black.
- He lives in a rough, inner-city part of London.
- He is described as 'a class clown, underachiever, shit-stirrer, playground loudmouth.'
- He shows little respect for teachers and is often in detention.
- He loves watching other boys fight, but never gets his own hands dirty.
- In Rugrat's world, being streetwise is more important than getting a good education.
- He is often very funny. Although some of his behaviour is questionable, he is strangely likable.
- Like a lot of young people, he wants to be popular and pretends to be tough. To what extent is this a front?
- Read the whole play to see what happens when Rugrat is forced to grow up and comes to a decision about what is right and what is wrong, thereby changing the course of his future.

FIVE THINGS TO HELP YOU PERFORM THE MONOLOGUE:

- You will need to capture that 'tough on the outside/soft on the inside' quality. Notice how, after getting angry about Baker and Jodie, he says, 'Still love her though'.
- See if you can imagine everything he describes: the other characters, the school, the corner where he kisses her, the physical sensation of that kiss, his hand on her thighs, the launderette and the bus, etc. The more detail you can bring to these pictures, the more depth the monologue will have.

- See if you can get a very strong sense of 'Joanne/Jodie's' split personality. Perhaps you know someone like that? How does it feel when they suddenly turn?
- Explore the different emotions in the monologue. One moment he is loved-up about Joanne, then the next he is angry and jealous about Baker. What might it feel like to be rejected for someone you consider your inferior?
- Make a decision about whether the crude language he uses is how he *really* feels about sex or just the way he thinks boys *should* talk. Interestingly, he is only crude when he describes Jodie and Baker together. When he remembers how it was between him and Joanne he speaks tenderly using words like 'patiently', 'bless' and 'nice'. You will also notice that he doesn't go into graphic detail, but just uses the word 'everything' leaving the rest to our own imagination.

Rugrat

“Four mornings out of five I'm late for school, guaranteed. I mean, they're lucky I even showed up to that ramshackle of a school anyway. When I'm really late, I see a whole group of different faces on the bus. Like this one girl, Jodie. She is so ridiculously buff? It's ridiculous. Gimme heartburn, that girl. She rocks the burgundy uniform cos she goes to EGA Sixth Form. That stands for Elizabeth Garrett Anderson but for us EGA stands for Every Girl Available. No one believes me but I kissed her one time, Jodie.

Swear down – on my mum's life. Before I even started secondary school.

'Twas the summer holiday before Year 7. Who do I see riding her bike through my area? Jodie, the queen of buffness. Courage from within took surface and I told her to stop and then I told her I wanna kiss her round the corner, so she walked her bike round the corner, where I was waiting patiently.

When we kissed her name was Joanne – and she was bless. But school made her remix it to Jodie; her evil side. *Joanne* was nice though. I had my hands on her cold thighs and everything.

When my washing machine broke down I got to see her at the launderette. She used to gel her hair down to her forehead – and it would come down to the side like this – (*Demonstrates.*) Fuck me though, was Jodie rude? That girl was roo-oode! Rude! No one could tell her nothing, boi. She didn't even have to touch you, she'll just drop you one line that'll feel like a t'ump in da face.

One time she roasted this woman on the bus for no reason. No reason! In front of everyone. The woman, all the woman did was ask Jodie politely, to put out her cigarette –

'Who the fuck are you with your penguin shoes, don't chat to me with your breath smelling like wet ass-crack… rah rah rah.'

Motormouth Jodie.

I was pissed when she started going out with Baker. Baker ya know. She had her pick of anyone in the world and she chooses him? He was the dumbest guy in our year. No one will ever truly know how dumb this guy was unless they was in our year. He came out with stupid shit, every single day – of his life. He had dumbness on tap. After a while it just stopped being funny cos, I mean, how can someone be so consistently dumb? Jodie went with him of all people, virginity and everything. Bareback – no protection. Watch Baker come into school the next day walking sideways, talking about his leg is hurting –

'She banged me, bruv, she banged me.'

I was P I doubled. I would've banged her properly. Cos thing is, if you know Baker you know he would've just lied there.

Bitch.

Still love her though. ”

Moth

Declan Greene

TEN THINGS YOU NEED TO KNOW ABOUT SEBASTIAN:

- Sebastian is fifteen years old.
- In the original version he is Australian, however the writer says that you can change this to make him come from wherever you do.
- He lives with his mum, who is a single parent. She has recently split up with her boyfriend.
- Sebastian is skinny, gawky and has bug-eyes, a shaved head and spotty skin.
- He wears a second-hand school blazer that is several sizes too big, trousers that are too short, and a shirt with no tie.
- He has really bad body odour and drowns himself in Lynx to try to disguise it.
- Sebastian has a really annoying laugh.
- He is obsessed with video games and post-apocalyptic anime – *Ghost in the Shell, Neon Genesis Evangelion, Akira, Trinity Blood,* etc.
- His only friend is a girl called Claryssa. Both he and Claryssa are considered weird and struggle to fit in. They are bullied at school. Theirs is a love-hate relationship. They enjoy mocking and swearing at one another, and Claryssa can be violent with him.
- The play is a two-hander in which Sebastian and Claryssa act out all the other characters.

FIVE THINGS TO HELP YOU PERFORM THE MONOLOGUE:

- The playwright tells us: '*Moth* is set within the memory of a specific time frame. Both Sebastian and Claryssa help enact each other's recollections.' In this sense the play is non-naturalistic. It is really important that you read the whole play to understand its dreamlike nature. This will allow you to grasp the monologue, which at first may seem a bit strange. The style is cartoon-like or fantastic, much like the video games that Sebastian plays.

- The monologue that follows describes the moment that St Sebastian appears to Sebastian demanding that he save the souls of all humanity. Before this happened Sebastian was being beaten up by the bullies at school who saw him kissing Claryssa. It is important to consider that in Sebastian's mind, he is propelled from 'zero to hero' as soon as the vision appears. It gives him purpose, strength and allows him to feel superhuman.
- The language is heightened, dramatic and poetic. See if you can revel in its muscularity. You cannot mumble a speech like this, but take care that you don't start shouting until perhaps you get to the very last line in capital letters. How does St Sebastian speak? Have fun impersonating him.
- The speech is highly descriptive. Create for yourself strong and vivid images, from the initial appearance of St Sebastian, all the way through to the arrival of the moths.
- Think about ways of connecting to the 'superhero' element. Do you ever fantasise about having special powers? Or about being able to save mankind from destruction? It may seem a bit far-fetched, and maybe these are things you remember from childhood, but see if you can make your own unique connection to the idea of good conquering evil. If you are not particularly into video games, perhaps you can draw upon science-fiction stories and films such as *Batman*, *Spider-Man*, *Superman* or *X-Men*, etc., for inspiration.

Sebastian

“This explosion, the back of my head…

I’m falling back, feel myself falling… I’m gonna hit the ground..

Pause.

But I don’t. […]

I don’t hit the ground. I just keep falling… Falling through light – this amazing warm light – this – tingling – […] – at the base of my spine. […] Pouring all through me – […] And this… This is when he appears.

– ‘Sebastian.’

Hanging in the light. A hundred feet tall. Bigger than I can even see. Plated in this, like, mecha-armour… Steam hissing out from the joints. He looks mostly android, I guess – but his chest is open, all meat and blood… Sick. A pair of lungs, filling with fluid. A heart beating in hot blue flame.

I know his name.

‘Sebastian.’

Same as my name.

‘My sweet child. Sebastian.’

And I’ve never been so scared in my life.

‘Do not be scared. I will not harm you.’

‘Are you an angel?’

‘I am St Sebastian – the nineteenth angel. Harbinger of a bitter prophecy.’

‘Are you my guardian angel?’

‘No. I am a destroying angel.’

‘Whoa. That’s… really, really sweet.’

‘I have come to you with a task, Sebastian. A wonderful and terrible task.’

'For me?'

'Yes, Sebastian. For you. Especially for you.'

And the port in the back of my spine tingles.

'Soon I am to descend. And your world is to be destroyed.'

And then I see it. I actually see it all. There's fire raining from the sky. People in the streets, eaten with flames, screaming as they burn. Rats streaming around their feet, rats fleeing –

'What is this?'

'This is Holy fire. The flame that cleanses.'

'Why are you showing me this?'

'This is your destiny. To save mankind. To usher them into the safe and awaiting arms of the Lord.'

'But how? What do I do?'

'You will know.'

And then – it starts to split… It flickers like a TV, like a billion globes are burning out – 'No, I don't know anything! I'm really dumb. I've never got better than a C-plus. Please!'

A burst of static.

'Have faith, Sebastian. This is a desperate world. But even in these darkest of times, there is still hope for mankind.'

'No, but what do I do? – What do I do?'

'You are that hope, Sebastian. You alone are pure enough for this solemn task.'

'Wait! – Sebastian? Sebastian?!' […] But everything falls apart…

An electrical charge: flickering, building in intensity.

St Sebastian breaks into a trillion tiny pieces, these pieces of light, flapping against the dark. And they're screaming. And they're all around me. Clouds of dust rise as they swarm…

Moths.

A trillion moths all around me. Smacking against my face, in my nostrils, crawling and crunching against one another… I try to scream – I try to scream but they pour in my mouth – they pour down my throat – filling my chest – and I cannot breathe, I try to gag, the dust, the dust, I cannot breathe I cannot scream I cannot breathe I close my eyes I cannot breathe I cannot breathe I cannot breathe I CANNOT I CANNOT I CANNOT I CANNOT – ”

My Boy Jack

David Haig

TEN THINGS YOU NEED TO KNOW ABOUT JOHN:

- The year is 1915, and John is eighteen.
- He is the son of the writer Rudyard Kipling, who is most famous for writing *The Jungle Book.*
- John is described as being tall, gangly and short-sighted. Out of context is doesn't matter what he looks like as long as he is short-sighted.
- John comes from an upper-middle-class background and speaks with an RP accent.
- He has an older sister called Elsie. His other sister called Josephine died of pneumonia when she was only six years old.
- John is a second lieutenant in the Irish Guards.
- John has been sent on a mission to France to fight the Germans during the First World War.
- Strictly speaking, John should not be fighting because of his severe myopia. However, despite failing several medical tests, John's father pulled some strings and secured John this position.
- Rudyard Kipling was a great advocate for the war, and some might say he bullied his son into joining up. In the play it is clear that John wants to fight, but it is less because he wants to defend his country, and more because he needs to escape the family home which he says is dark, depressing and suffocating.
- John is a sensitive young man. He is not aggressive and is therefore vulnerable.

FIVE THINGS TO HELP YOU PERFORM THE MONOLOGUE:

- You will need to do some research into the First World War and the appalling conditions the soldiers endured in the trenches. I would suggest reading the novel *Birdsong* by Sebastian Faulks. In it there is a brilliant and unrelenting description of what life was like for these very young men, or 'cannon fodder' as they were known.
- John is in charge of leading his men into battle. For one they do not respect him, and for another, he is ill-equipped to do so. The monologue comes moments before 'zero hour', the point at which the charge is to be led. You will need to capture this feeling of being on the edge of a void, or a big unknown. Although it does not carry the same danger, you could equate it to that sick feeling you get before you go on stage. Have you ever waited on the side of the stage terrified of forgetting your lines, but then entering as soon as your cue is called as though you are on autopilot? Perhaps you can draw on this sensation in order to connect to John's terror. If you times it by a thousand you might have an idea of what John is going through.
- I have included the stage directions that precede and conclude the speech. It will be useful to create some context by taking your glasses off before you start the monologue. In this way you can show John's vulnerability and how ill-equipped he is for battle. Ending the speech looking at your watch and then blowing a whistle will create a fine finish. Think about what you will use to represent the pistol (see note on using props in the introduction). Remember that it is raining, which adds to the atmosphere of hopelessness and doom.
- It is as if John is practising or going over what he has been taught to do before the actual point of Zero Hour. It will be helpful to physicalise these movements or manoeuvres as you describe them. Again, you may find it useful to think about what you do before you go on stage. Perhaps you go over your lines once more. Perhaps you practise some move or business with a prop. How will you connect to that feeling of having prepared or rehearsed something so well that when it finally comes there is no going back?

- In his state of terror it is his family that he misses the most. 'Daddo' is the name he calls his father and Elsie is his beloved sister. The Alhambra is the name of a theatre where they will have seen a play after supper. It is poignant that, having joined the army to escape his family, in his final moments John is recalling them for comfort. Read the whole play to find out what happened to John Kipling.

John

" JOHN *takes off his glasses a final time and dries them.*

I'm *so* frightened.

My heart is beating everywhere, behind my eyes, down my legs, in my chest… pulsing, hammering.

It's cold.

Please God I mustn't let them down. Will I be brave? Will I fail? – Onto the firestep – keep the pistol out of the mud – left hand on the parapet – pull – right foot on the sand bags – push up – left leg over – Straighten – run – I mustn't let them down. Some of these men will be dead tonight. I may be dead tonight. Let me live. Stop raining – just for a second.

Oh Daddo – what luxury – to turn on a hot water tap – hot steaming water – evening clothes – dinner at The Ritz – the Alhambra afterwards. Elsie. Mother. Daddo. – My first action – Fifteen seconds – is that the whistle? – one clear blast – left hand – parapet – sand bags – over – run. Run fast and straight. Please God let me live. Pistol high – run, run, run.

JOHN *looks at his watch. Zero Hour. He blows his whistle.* "

Natives

Glenn Waldron

TEN THINGS YOU NEED TO KNOW ABOUT **b.**:

- Today is his fourteenth birthday.
- His brother has died and he is at his funeral.
- He comes from an underprivileged background and lives, as he calls it, in a 'nothing town'.
- He has no expectation of doing well at school or bettering himself.
- He has little respect for those in authority.
- His day-to-day life is dominated by media images of violence and pornography.
- Like a lot of young men, he feels a pressure to look and act tough and to treat women like objects.
- None of his brother's friends have come to the funeral. His mother is unable to give him support, and despite his 'bravado' we get the impression that he is scared and lonely.
- His precise heritage or ethnicity is unspecified, so he can be played by someone who looks like you.
- Despite the peer pressure, he is surprisingly individual. When you read the whole play, you will see that he has the potential to break free from the crowd.

FIVE THINGS TO HELP YOU PLAY THE MONOLOGUE:

- Give yourself a name. Although the playwright calls him 'b.', it will help you to understand/feel closer to him if you know what he is called.
- Think about his accent and the way he speaks. Although he can be played by any nationality, it is important that you

capture the fact that he is a poor kid and speaks in that defensive way that kids who have been neglected often do.

- See if you can imagine what the vicar looks like and how it feels to be in the church.
- The video he is watching is violent and sexually charged. How does that make him feel while at the same time seeing his brother in a coffin? Perhaps the anger he feels at the loss of his brother is being channelled into what he can see on his phone.
- He cannot/does not know how to cry, but he is hurting inside. Find a way of playing tough on the outside but sad on the inside. We often cover our emotions by pretending that everything is normal or fine. Maybe something similar has happened to you or you have experienced the need to hide your true feelings. Decide to what extent b. is covering *his* pain and grief by shutting out what is actually going on around him.

NB This play offers a number of other monologues from which to choose.

b.

“I’m watching this thing on my phone and the old guy opposite me’s giving me evils.

He’s one of these Harry Potter-headmaster types and he’s giving me real evils.

And – and I’m looking at him like, alright, chill.

What’s your problem, dude? Relax.

No biggie, mate.

No one’s died.

And I mean, technically that’s not true.

Technically we’re at a funeral and – and technically he’s the vicar.

But, y'know, not really a problem, is it?

Not really hurting anyone, is it?

And because, what am I meant to do?

Listen to old Dumbledore bang on about the Gospel of the Good Samaritan?

You're alright.

You're good. [...]

He's giving me evils, old Dumbledore, and then they're doing some hymn.

Some really boring, crappy hymn.

Something about *ploughing the seed and scattering*.

I mean, What The Actual, yeah?

And I put my earphones in and go back to what I'm watching.

The thing I'm watching on my phone.

It's this film about this Japanese gangster.

He's a Japanese gangster but he also happens to be a cannibal.

But then one day, he, like, decides to be good, yeah?

And instead of just killing Japanese men for money, he decides to rescue all these women.

All these super-fit Japanese women.

Only sometimes, on account of his innate cannibalistic nature, the temptation's too much and he accidentally eats them.

He accidentally eats all the super-fit Japanese women.

It's sick, man.

It's really sick! ❞

Natives

Glenn Waldron

TEN THINGS YOU NEED TO KNOW ABOUT C.:

- Today is his fourteenth birthday.
- He comes from a country in the Middle East, like Syria or Iraq.
- His country has been at war, but now things are safer and people are attempting to get back to normal.
- He lives with his mum and dad who are very strict.
- He has sisters and an older brother called Ali whom he looks up to.
- He is obsessed with video games and can't wait to play *Hiro's Kingdom 5*, which his brother Ali has given to him as a birthday present.
- Like a lot of young boys and girls whose lives have been dominated by war, he has been forced to witness things no child should see. In this way he is old before his time.
- Many of his friends, including his brother, have been desensitised by the horrors of war. They have lost their sense of compassion and are capable of extreme cruelty.
- However, despite extreme peer pressure, c. has managed to remain sensitive and is able to think for himself.
- Read the whole play to find out what happens when c. has the opportunity to make a stand.

FIVE THINGS TO HELP YOU PLAY THE MONOLOGUE:

- Give yourself a name. Although the playwright calls him 'c.', it will help you to understand/feel closer to him if you know what he is called.
- You will need to have or be able to do a Middle-Eastern or Arab accent.

- Think about how playful he is (having a laugh about someone farting), and then how serious he can be (understanding the complex politics of his country). See if you can capture this journey from a happy teenager to a pupil who thinks deeply.
- Although he refuses to follow the herd and simply believe what he is told, he is afraid to step out of line. This shows a respect for authority, but it also tells you something about the fear that is dominant in his society.
- See if you can imagine what the teacher, the schoolroom and the other pupils look like. How might it differ from your own experience of being in school?

NB This play offers a number of other monologues from which to choose.

c.

" Yasin has just farted!

It's the second lesson of the day and it's history.

And everyone is looking in Yasin's direction because he's just done this really big, wet-sounding fart.

Like – (*Makes the sound of the fart.*)

And you don't want to smell it, you really don't want to smell it but then – argh! – you also don't want to be left out.

Also a fart is actually just a combination of nitrogen, hydrogen, carbon dioxide, methane and oxygen, so how bad can it be?

And you don't want to smell it. But then you sort of do.

Just to see how bad it is.

And so you do.

You sort of sniff and –

It's nothing.

It's nothing really.

It's not a good smell but it's not that bad, it's nothing like the sound but then –

Oh!

Oh my life.

It hits you.

Oh!

A wave of the nastiest, dirtiest, most toxic smell you have ever smelt.

Ever.

It is off the scale!

Like, if you made a chart of all the bad smells in the world, then you'd need extra paper and some tape to show where it is on the chart.

Oh!

Like the smell of a rotting sheep carcass mixed with your grandfather's bad breath and then, and then a bag of seven-day-old rubbish. All rolled into one… and then made worse!

It is so bad that it is actually quite incredible.

Incredible that someone has made this, that the insides of someone's body has made this smell.

And everyone's kind of going crazy and like coughing, and like looking at each other, and pretending to gasp for air.

But then the teacher's ignoring it and it's beginning to disperse.

And the teacher's talking about the Glorious History of this Country.

Of this city.

And the teacher's saying all this stuff and –

And some of it makes sense and that's good but then –

Some of it doesn't – hang together.

There's bits missing.

There's definitely bits missing.

And he's saying how lucky you are, lucky *we* are to be on the good side.

How lucky we were to fight off the rebels. The terrorists.

And everyone's writing it down.

They're all writing that down.

And then you're wondering if everyone thinks they're on the good side.

If everyone everywhere thinks that too.

If anyone ever thinks they're on the bad side.

And, like, maybe some people *are* on the good side.

Like Hiro. Like Hiro in *Hiro's Kingdom.*

But maybe sometimes they're just on the side that wins.

Maybe sometimes it's not the good side but just the side that wins.

And how the people in the city, the people in the other city called your city the rebels.

Called you the terrorists.

And then you're thinking about this family.

And even though they are a Western family and, like, a cartoon family, they are just like your family.

They really are!

And you think how the cartoon family don't go to prayers or eat the food you eat or even speak the language you speak but how the cartoon family are sort of like your family too.

And you think, which side are the yellow family on? Which side are the yellow cartoon family on?

And that's what you're thinking when the teacher asks if anyone has any questions.

Which side are the cartoon family actually on?

You don't ask the teacher that though.

Of course you don't ask the teacher that though. ”

Plastic

Kenneth Emson

This play deals with adult themes. It has content and language that some readers might find disturbing or offensive.

TEN THINGS YOU NEED TO KNOW ABOUT KEV:

- Kev is nineteen.
- He comes from a small town along the Thames Estuary in Essex.
- When he was still at school he was captain of the school football team and scored the winning goal in the All-Essex Schools Cup Final.
- He is considered 'a bit hard'.
- He drives a fast car.
- He smokes weed and Benson & Hedges cigarettes.
- All the pretty girls fancy him.
- He fancies a girl called Lisa. She is only fifteen and still a virgin.
- Kev still lives at home with his mum.
- He has a dead-end job stacking shelves.

FIVE THINGS TO HELP YOU PERFORM THE MONOLOGUE:

- Kev's accent is important. This is a play set firmly in Essex and what is known as an Estuary English accent is part of the music of the piece. I wouldn't suggest changing it. However, if you really love the speech and can't do the accent, make sure you choose something that fits in with his background.
- Although the language is contemporary, it is also heightened, poetic and rhythmic. This gives the play a muscularity, as if the language is a kind of heartbeat, pulsating and creating urgency and dramatic tension. Enjoy speaking it, searching out the

rhythms and rhymes. Although it must be realistic, it is not the kind of monologue that should be mumbled or thrown away.

- Think about what Lisa looks and sounds like. Kev describes her as 'young and pretty… too pretty for me', and at fifteen she is significantly younger than Kev. She is, of course, underage, and although he is only nineteen he is still the 'older man'. How does she make you feel? Perhaps you too have been attracted to a younger girl and have been flattered by her response. What does it feel like when you receive her text? Think about how her giving you the 'green light' in this way sets up the sexual tension for both characters.
- After the glory of his football schooldays, Kev feels like a failure. He knows that he hasn't reached his potential, but he lacks drive and ambition. The fact that Lisa wants him allows him to feel special again. Through her he can forget about his failures and his disappointments.
- Think about your physicality. When you are so attracted to someone, you become physically restless. He can't wait for the moment and smokes a spliff to steady himself. Perhaps you know that feeling or have observed it in someone else. Either way it is important that you connect to his mounting state of excitement when performing the monologue.

Kev

“ Lids open
Sun's up already
Curtains split
By the human alarm clock
That is my old tit.
Clock gives it that I'm late
Give it right back.
Blue skies
Be no work today
Reebok Classic of a day today.
Morning radio chirps out

Some banging
Two-step sounds
And the day beginneth. […]

Pick up my phone
To bleat the usual excuse
Of bad stomachs
From bad kebabs
From bad night outs
In bad streets.
But the phone's started up without me
Bleeping its bleep in my hand
Ignoring my finger's request.

And it's her.

The one thing that saves this life
From being just another
Bad cover
Of all the other lads that grew round here
Before I.
In capital letters she speaks to me
Important like.
And it's the news
'TODAY'S THE DAY'
She says
Today's the day
Yes it is
Reebok Classic of a day today
Yes.
It.
Is. […]

Scrape myself from the bed
Sky's up there smiling
Warm and righteous.
Don't get better than this.
'Part from the cherry-balmed linger
Left from the taste of her kiss […]

Sat on the sofa in yesterday's boxers.

Ignoring my own smell wafting up
And stinking at my nose.
Roll a spliff
Slim-skinned Rizla shakes in my hand
Steady.
I'm ready.
And toke.
Stopping the day and anything it can throw. [...]

'Bout ten start to think about [...]

Today [...]

Can't come quick enough [...]

This is it [...]

The girls that stank up my fingers
On nights when I was meant to be home
Learning.
So I don't end up being
What I end up being
Ain't meaning shit to me now. [...]

Reebok Classic of a day [...]

No more pretending [...]

No [...]

And I'm thinking... [...]

Need some johnnies [...]

Want this to be perfect [...]

Want this to be better...[...]

Than anything else. ”

Precious Little Talent

Ella Hickson

TEN THINGS YOU NEED TO KNOW ABOUT SAM:

- Sam is nineteen.
- He is American.
- He lives in New York.
- He works as a carer.
- His client is man called George, who suffers from dementia.
- His ambition is to be a doctor.
- Sam moved to New York when he was only sixteen, and every night he would repeat to himself: 'If you're going to make your way in the world, it's going to take everything you've got'.
- He says he believes in 'God, my country, my family… Myself'.
- He is an optimist.
- He is romantic.

FIVE THINGS TO HELP YOU PERFORM THE MONOLOGUE:

- Sam is talking to the audience (see note on talking to the audience in the introduction). He is excited and desperate to share his story.
- In the monologue he also talks to Joey, the girl he has just met and fallen in love with. Perhaps you know that feeling of love at first sight. Let it overwhelm you.
- Imagine what Joey looks like. Perhaps you could personalise her as someone you already know.
- If you have never been to New York, research the places that he mentions. You might like to watch the film *Breakfast at Tiffany's.*

- The monologue has an element of fantasy about it, as if it were a dream come true. Have fun with it.

Sam

“ It's Christmas Eve in the winter of two thousand eight and the night is cruel and beautiful and it feels like it's the first time it's ever been that way. I'm sitting on a rooftop, downtown New York City; in front of me midtown, pouring out into the night like a million luminous toothpicks, but right around me is black, black and death. I'm nineteen and I've got an erection, right tight into the front of my pants 'cos I can feel a woman's breath on the left side of my neck. This nervous little breath, panting, just beneath my ear; the moisture in it licking at me in the dark night and I so desperately want to turn around and suck that in, so desperately – but I keep my hands on my thighs, just like this and I say 'hey'.

[…] (*To* JOEY.) What's your name?

[…] No shit, mine too!

[…] No, it's Sam. I'm sorry – I don't know why I just said that.

(*To audience.*) She laughs this funny little laugh and it sounds funny so I say – You sound funny. […]

She says, all like that, all 'I'm English', like that. (*To* JOEY.) […] So… you're up here for, um – a little air? […]

(*To audience.*) So I'm thinking 'a little air', like taking a turn on the veranda, like a midnight, moonlit stroll, like Audrey Hepburn at dawn before breakfast time at Tiffany's; like this is the moment you might tell your kids that you met and she says – […]

(*To* JOEY.) Hepburn? […]

How did you do that? […]

(*To audience.*) And then I'm sure you won't believe this, I'm sure you will have heard this said a thousand times before but piano music starts to play. [...]

And suddenly we're running fast as our feet will take us, stamping down fire escapes, looking in on late-night offices where tired and desperate men are sitting and watching dollars dropping like flies but we're running, fast and quick and furious. We're headed down Bleecker where the lights are kind and the windows are crowded up with smart stuff and slutty stuff and it's cold, you see, so cold that my fingers get numb so as they might be tempted to let go of the very best thing that they have ever had the pleasure of holding on to –

(*To* JOEY.) You want to take the subway? [...]

(*To audience.*) We take the uptown 6 train that goes all the way up and down Manhattan, scratching its back along the side of Central Park – we take it all the way up through Astor and Union and 59th and 96th and all the way on up to Harlem and when we get to the top we just come right back again and on our way back down we just can't stop looking at each other and we laugh and we put our hands over our faces like kids in a bathtub – [...]

I take her hand and I lead her off that train and I've judged my timing right because we emerge right into the middle of Grand Central Station. [...]

And do you know what I did – right then, right in the middle of Grand Central Station? I pulled her right around and I kissed her, real hard. And when I stopped, when I stopped and stood back and I looked at her, she said the strangest thing, she said... 'I don't believe in you.' ”

Rabbit Hole

David Lindsay-Abaire

TEN THINGS YOU NEED TO KNOW ABOUT JASON:

- Jason is seventeen.
- He comes from Larchmont, which is a fairly prosperous suburb of New York.
- He lives with his mother.
- We are given to understand that his father, who was an English teacher, is dead.
- He says he is the only one at home now, so we assume that he has an older brother and/or sister.
- Eight months ago, while driving his car, he killed a four-year-old boy who ran into the road after his dog.
- He is racked with guilt as he thinks he may have been going slightly faster than the speed limit.
- He used to have a girlfriend, but they broke up.
- He wants to be a writer, and is about to leave home to study at Connecticut College.
- He is particularly interested in science fiction and believes strongly in the existence of parallel universes.

FIVE THINGS TO HELP YOU PERFORM THE MONOLOGUE:

- As you can tell, the monologue is a letter that Jason has written to the parents of Danny, the four-year-old boy. You may like to practise the speech at a desk as if you were writing. When you come to perform it, however, you could just speak it as if you were talking directly to Mr and Mrs Corbett. See if you can picture what they look like and direct your focus there.
- The guilt Jason feels won't go away. He is particularly troubled by the fact that he may have been doing more than the speed

limit. Although you probably won't have felt such intense guilt, you may be able to connect to this feeling of having done something wrong which still bothers you. Even if it is a small thing in comparison, see if you can amplify it to try to understand how Jason might be feeling.

- The need to meet with the boy's parents is born out of a strong desire to get their forgiveness. Let this need for forgiveness drive the speech.
- The 'ha ha'. I would suggest playing these as if you were actually laughing (rather than saying the words 'ha ha'). There is something pathetic about Jason's attempts at a joke, and perhaps it is more of a nervous laughter than an actual guffaw.
- How might you visualise Danny and his parents? He will have a memory of the accident itself. What will he have remembered from that day? His mother was at home, so he would have seen her and we know that there have been pictures of the family in the newspaper. See if you can form a visual narrative of the accident in your head (as usual, read the whole play), and how you wished you had not taken that route. When something bad happens, we are usually haunted by the events, and it is obvious that Jason can't stop picturing it. It could be that it is like a film inside his head that is played and rewound, and then played again, as if on a loop.

Jason

“Dear Mr and Mrs Corbett,

I wanted to send you my condolences on the death of your son, Danny. I know it's been eight months since the accident, but I'm sure it's probably still hard for you to be reminded of that day. I think about what happened a lot, as I'm sure you do, too. I've been having some troubles at home, and at school, and a couple people here thought it might be a good idea to write to you. I'm sorry if this letter upsets you. That's obviously not my intention.

Even though I never knew Danny, I did read that article in the town paper, and was happy to learn a little bit about him. He sounds like he was a great kid. I'm sure you miss him a lot, as you said in the article. I especially liked the part where Mr Corbett talked about Danny's robots, because when I was his age I was a big fan of robots, too. In fact I still am, in some ways – ha ha.

I've enclosed a short story that's going to be printed in my high-school lit magazine. I don't know if you like science fiction or not, but I've enclosed it anyway. I was hoping to dedicate the story to Danny's memory. There aren't any robots in this one, but I think it would be the kind of story he'd like if he were my age. Would it bother you if I dedicated the story? If so, please let me know. The printer deadline for the magazine is March 31st. If you tell me before then, I can have them take it off.

I know this probably doesn't make things any better, but I wanted you to know how terrible I feel about Danny. I know that no matter how hard this has been on me, I can never understand the depth of your loss. My mom has only told me that about a hundred times – ha ha. I of course wanted to say how sorry I am that things happened the way they did, and that I wish I had driven down a different block that day. I'm sure you do, too.

Anyway, that's it for now. If you'd like to let me know about the dedication, you can email me at the address above. If I don't hear from you, I'll assume it's okay.

Sincerely, Jason Willette

Beat.

PS Would it be possible to meet you in person at some point? ”

Run

Stephen Laughton

This play deals with adult themes. It has content and language that some readers might find disturbing or offensive.

TEN THINGS YOU NEED TO KNOW ABOUT YONNI:

- Yonni is seventeen.
- He is a Jewish boy from Hendon in north London.
- He lives with his mum Devorah, father Reuben and younger brother Jesse.
- Yonni is gay.
- His family are religious. They are Sephardi Jews, which means they originally come from countries such as Spain and Portugal.
- He is sensitive and has numerous allergies.
- Although he is clever, he prefers to hang out with the boys who like to smoke, cramming for exams at the last minute.
- He is funny, often rebellious, and swears a lot.
- He is a good cook and loves listening to 'Trap Queen' by Fetty Wap.
- When you have read the whole play you will understand how brave he is.

FIVE THINGS TO HELP YOU PLAY THE MONOLOGUE:

- Yonni is in love with Adam. Perhaps you have experienced a similar attraction, in which case you can draw on these sensations when performing the monologue. Adam is an Ashkenazi Jew, which means his heritage is Russian or Polish. He lives in Gants Hill which is on the other side of London, in the east.

- You will need to hold a very strong image of him in your mind's eye. We know he is fair-haired. Perhaps you know someone who looks like him, or, if not, you can paint your own picture from your imagination.
- Get a picture in your head about how your mum and younger brother look. What would they be wearing? Also think about the group of schoolkids. Are they in school uniform? What does the playground look like? The more you can visualise these little details, the more you will bring the monologue to life.
- There are many transitions in the monologue. Think about how you will go from mucking around with your friends to the moment when you spot Adam, and then, from being left alone with Adam to the arrival of your mother, her 'raging' and the deep embarrassment that you feel. Remember that throughout all of this Adam remains focused on you.
- The language has a particular dynamic and sometimes there is an almost-rhyme, such as 'disarming' and 'calming'. Notice the way there are some very short sentences with several full stops and then longer sentences where Yonni's thoughts are more fluid. See if you can use the language as a kind of clue to how he is feeling. He is shy with Adam and thinks in short sentences, but then annoyed at his mother, venting his rage in much longer sentences.

NB This play offers a number of other monologues from which to choose.

Yonni

" It's muck-up day today…
And the Year 11s, me and mine, get to bolt after next period…

Study leave.

Or as we like to call it 'getting stoned with your mates all week then fully cramming with the geeky kids you've hung shit on for the last four years the night of your modular science exam'.

Then passing.

And there's buzzing and manoeuvring and rowdiness in the air.

The kids in my year all excited 'bout egg and flour and maybe the odd firework. Some kid trying to convince us to catapult chickens at the school walls.

I hope they're kosher.

And in the rabble I spot you.

Smiling, cool, somewhat removed…

Soaking it up…

Like, the day after we met, like properly… At that bus stop…

And you're standing there….

Like. Grinning…
Like that.

Hot.

Blue-green eyes.
Messy hair. Cute smile.

You're fair.
Not like me.
Intellectual. Less like me.
A nice Ashkenazi boy.

You're deep. Literal… Something of the artist…
Bit more like me…

Watching it all unfold.

Then you spot me.
Nod.
And I freeze.

Eyes locked.

One…
Two…

And I brave it.

Walk over.

Leave my mates behind as they head off for whatever little juvenile ploy they'll play…

Then it's us. Alone.

Hey. You say.

And it's fully disarming.
Kinda calming.

But before we even get to say another thing I look up and there she is.

Devorah.

Raging.

In the middle of the playground.
Dragging Jesse behind her…

And I freeze and she's instantly all over me ordering that we leave and I'm like *NO* no way *it's my last day* but she's having none of it she's not coming back and I'm telling her I can make my own way home and everyone's watching and she's like don't answer back and everyone's watching and she tells me we're leaving and before I can argue and everyone's watching I'm warned that I better not start as well.

And everyone's watching.

And I'm horrified.

And we lock eyes, you and I, and you mouth to me… ask me if I'm alright.

And the whole thing seems to swim…

As everyone's watching.

And in the –

Shame.
That rises.
The the the panic… that rises…

You hold me.
With your gaze.

And as as as I'm lead away….

Head down… whispering frantically to Devorah about how embarrassing she is, not really paying attention to her total eppy about her meeting with the Head and Jesse and his Hebrew teacher Mr Weiner and how Reuben is probably gonna go batshit crazy –

You catch up.

Pull me back for a second and I'm torn between you and Devorah, glance back at her as you pull out a pen… start to write on my arm… I guess it's muck-up day, so it's kinda what you do and she's calling me back and I pull away.

Smile. Apologetically.

Clock what you've written.

And exhale.
Realise I've been holding my breath.

Adam.
07590 –
And I commit it to –

Stop.

And blur.

Later. ❞

Scuttlers

Rona Munro

TEN THINGS YOU NEED TO KNOW ABOUT THOMAS:

- Thomas is a teenage slum-dweller. He has been living on the streets in Ancoats, Manchester.
- The year is 1882.
- Thomas is described as being 'bright, energetic and friendly'. He is the kind of person who is more on the outside of the action and desperate to fit in.
- Thomas is a really good dancer, which has attracted the attention of the ladies and annoyed some of the men.
- He doesn't have a permanent job and so picks up whatever manual labour is going.
- He is good at stealing things without anyone noticing.
- Because he is from Chorlton, which is outside the city centre, it has taken a while but he has finally been accepted into a gang called The Tigers of Bengal Street. Thomas's ambition is to be 'King' of the gang one day.
- Thomas is a scuttler, which was the name given to gang members who ruled the streets in Manchester in the late-nineteenth century.
- The gang's greatest enemy is the Prussia Street mob, with whom they have called for a fight.
- It is a hot summer, the factories are closed but the pubs have been open. Fuelled by drink and restless from unemployment, Thomas and the others are ready for a fight.

FIVE THINGS TO HELP YOU PERFORM THE MONOLOGUE:

- Thomas is talking to Theresa, also a teenage slum-dweller. Theresa has taken pity on Thomas and has let him share her bed. See if you can imagine the cramped lodging house that she shares with several others.

- They are talking about their mothers, playing a kind of a game to see whose mother was the most stupid.
- Thomas and Theresa are drinking gin. Without playing drunk, you might like to reference the fact by playing the monologue while taking occasional sips from a bottle.
- Thomas is really attracted to Theresa. She is the kind of girl who is tough on the outside but soft on the inside. See if you can imagine what she might look like.
- Think about how you are competing but also flirting with Theresa. By the end of their scene together, Thomas will kiss her.

Thomas

“ My mother, my mother was so stupid… she was so stupid she couldn’t have another kid without she had to find a split new dad for it.

She couldn’t remember my dad at all. One day she’s telling me he was working on the railway. The next she told me he’d gone up north…

I don’t think she liked my dad. I think she’d forgotten him altogether and then she saw him on my face and started remembering.

So whatever she remembered it must have made her angry…

So this one day I’ve thrown a stone at John the joiner next door. Not a big rock or anything, just a pebble, just for the fun of seeing him jump a bit, you know?

He says, ‘Why don’t you go and break windows and scuttle folk in Ancoats like your dad and leave decent folk their peace.’

And she took his side over mine.

And my big sister says she doesn't care if I never come home.

And my big brother never says a thing, just gives her half his wage and goes out like he's king of the house.

When I said I was going the only person that cried was my little sister.

I miss my little sister Martha.

She's good at the reading.

I were never good at reading. All the letters dance about, like they're playing a trick on me. [...]

He were the king of the street. [My dad.] Thomas Clayton. [...] I followed his name to Ancoats.

That's the only thing I'm sure of. 'I should never have given you his name,' she says, 'even his name's trouble.'

It's powerful trouble my name. I'm sure of that.

She should have loved me best. I were the only one of us that could dance.

She likely loved Martha best. You always love the littlest best, don't you? ”

Vernon God Little

Tanya Ronder
Adapted from DBC Pierre's novel

TEN THINGS YOU NEED TO KNOW ABOUT VERNON:

- Vernon is a fifteen-year-old schoolboy.
- He comes from a small town in Texas, USA.
- He is an only child.
- He lives with his mother, who is a single parent. She has a boyfriend, whom Vernon hates.
- Three years ago Vernon's father disappeared. He was presumed dead, although his body was never found. As we discover in the monologue that follows, Vernon's mother shot his father and in secret they buried the body.
- Vernon's father was violent, and Vernon and his mother would often be covered in bruises.
- Vernon's best friend Jesus has recently shot seventeen fellow schoolchildren in a high-school massacre before turning the gun on himself.
- The townspeople are angry and want someone to pay for the shootings. Vernon becomes the scapegoat and is wrongly accused of being Jesus's accomplice.
- Vernon, who suffers from unpredictable bowel movements, could not have helped Jesus at the time of the shooting because he was behind the gym defecating. However, Jesus left his bag of ammunition outside the classroom and Vernon was later found with it.
- Vernon is a quiet kind of regular kid, who allows himself to become a victim of circumstance, partly because he cannot speak up for himself, and partly because he is unsupported by the adults around him.

FIVE THINGS TO HELP YOU PERFORM THE MONOLOGUE:

- You will need to have an idea of the world of the play. It is set in a typical small town in America where people are arguably 'backward', 'Bible-bashing', violent, corrupt and lawless. Although set in the Midwest of America rather than Texas, recent films such as *Three Billboards Outside Ebbing, Missouri* are not dissimilar in atmosphere.
- Vernon is talking to his mother. Although she is on stage with him she is at home and cannot hear him. She is more interested in the arrival of her new refrigerator than the plight of her son. See if you can picture talking to your/Vernon's mother so that you can direct the speech to a real person in your imagination.
- Set somewhere between a courtroom and a cell on death row, this is the first time that Vernon has spoken out. Up until now his embarrassment over his bowel movements prevented him. However, here no one is listening. Imagine the loneliness he feels and the desperation of knowing you are innocent when found guilty.
- You will need to perform the speech in an American accent, preferably Texan or somewhere from the Southern States. 'Jesus' is a Mexican/Spanish name and is pronounced 'Hey-zoos', rather than the English 'Je-zus'.
- Although it is too late, Vernon wants to prove his innocence, confront his mother and reveal the truth about how his father died. He wants justice, and although a large part of him feels let down, he still needs his mother's love. Make sure you play these objectives as you chart your way through the speech.

Vernon

❝ The way he ran from class, I knew the storm was breaking in Jesus. He'd been wired for weeks, more ditzy than usual, calling it love but not saying who with… If you'd come to Houston, Mom, and been in court you'd have heard about the photo on the Doctor's website. That morning in math, this picture of Jesus in these stupid panties, was on every computer in the room. 'Bambi Boy Butt Bazaar'? He had no idea. He jackknifed. I asked Lori to cover for me because I knew where he was headed. I raced to Keeter's on my bike, to the den, where both our daddy's guns were. He wasn't there. The den was locked, my key at home. I saw through the crack in the door, Daddy's rifle was there, not moved since the day we left it, but his daddy's had gone. My turn to jackknife. Back on the bike, my insides cramped, what a surprise. Gastro-enteritis fuckin' Little. I squatted, emptied my lower tracts like rats from an airplane, right beside the den. 'Tell them about the poo-poos!' says my attorney, and he's right. They'd know I wasn't in school, then. You'd know I wasn't in school too, but what am I supposed to say? 'Sure, there's the shit, right beside my papa's grave where me an' Mom buried him in the middle of the fucking night after she shot him dead. And in case you're interested, the gun's right behind that corrugated door. The key? Sure – little box in my room – anything else I can help with?' My shit makes me innocent but it sure as hell would put you away. Seventeen children? How could you think I did that?

By the time I cleaned myself up, Jesus was at school with his pop's loaded rifle. I didn't get there in time. I found his bag outside the classroom, picked it up, held on to it. Inside was another round of ammunition beside his lunch – shrimp-paste on white. I looked through the door and there they all were – shot to pieces, and there was my goofy friend Jesus, with the gun pointing deep inside his mouth. ❞

What We Know

Pamela Carter

TEN THINGS YOU NEED TO KNOW ABOUT THE TEENAGER:

- The Teenager calls himself Lee, then Hank, and then Marvin – as in 'Starvin' Marvin' from *South Park*.
- His exact age is not specified. You can decide.
- He is Scottish. Although out of context he could come from another part of the UK.
- He says that he is an honest person and always tells the truth.
- Because he is still growing, he is permanently hungry. He has to eat regularly and says he likes both sweet and savoury dishes.
- The Teenager is cheeky. He likes to joke and to have a bit of banter.
- However, he is also quite well behaved and hates it when adults swear.
- In the play he is a mysterious figure who appears without warning, and then leaves just as randomly.
- We know nothing about his background.
- Use the opportunity to create a fully rounded character for yourself by filling in the blanks.

FIVE THINGS TO HELP YOU PERFORM THE MONOLOGUE:

- The Teenager is talking to a woman called Lucy. Earlier that evening, Lucy was preparing a meal with her partner Jo. As they were cooking, Jo mysteriously disappeared and moments later the Teenager appeared in his place. To the audience the teenager represents something strange and unknown. When Lucy asks him where he comes from he says, 'i dunno, the fairies left me'. However, you should portray him as ordinarily as possible.

- The Teenager is very hungry, and Lucy has made him a cheese sandwich. He tells her about the dead body in exchange for her feeding him. He says afterwards that he was just trying to make conversation and that she might like to hear a story. Take this as a note to keep the monologue light in tone despite its dark content. The teenager is clearly having fun telling the story, and you need to find the contrast between the gruesomeness of the dead body and the excitement the teenager experiences when he discovers it. As he says, it's like being in a film.
- The monologue is highly descriptive. Make sure that you can picture in your mind's eye all that he describes. Have an idea about what Lucy looks like. She's in her thirties.
- Strictly speaking, the Teenager is Scottish. If the Scottish accent is not native to you or you find it difficult to perform, you might like to try it in an accent that suits you. Make sure whatever you choose that it is a kind of ghetto or 'street speak' typical of many teenagers.
- You might find it interesting to consider why the writer has chosen to write the entire play in lower-case letters. Read the whole play to understand more fully how ordinary events take on a surreal significance.

Teenager

“you ever seen a dead body? […] i saw a dead body once.

[…] it was years ago back when i was young, right? and i'm playing out in these fields. and there's this stream with a pond, like, and a big pipe across it you can stand on. really big. massive. […]

so i'm sat up on this pipe and checking out the view. you know, sun's shining, sky's blue. and i'm looking in the pond, right?

[…]

cos people chuck random stuff in there or there are animals or cars, you know, and it's interesting. but sometimes no and it's just rubbish and so i'm having a butcher's and i see this dummy, you know? like a dummy from a shop. and i think 'oh look, someone's thrown a dummy in here.'

but then, there's this moment, right? really radical. [...] you know, when you look at something and it's one thing and then you're still looking at it and it's not that thing any more; it's the same but then it's totally different? same – different. same – different. you with me?

[...] so one minute i'm looking at a dummy like from a shop, you know. and the next minute, it's a woman.

a real woman. a real dead woman. [...] and it's really freaky, man, because I know that she's like dead just like in a film. and it's not a film because it's real but it is like a film because everything's a bit slow-motion-y and a bit woooo.

it's like i'm a camera and i'm zooming in and out, you know, on this dead woman. like she's getting bigger and then smaller. close up and then far away, you know. oooooop and then waaaaay. do you know what i'm saying?

[...]

it's wild cos like i can do it now. like the whole thing's like my own personal film in my own head and i can like freeze it and go 'oooooop' and then 'waaaaay'. in my own head. well cool.

well, not for her. cos she was dead. it wasn't cool for her or anything, obviously. because that would be sick, like. not right.

[...]

extreme stuff. awesome. ”

Wink

Phoebe Eclair-Powell

TEN THINGS YOU NEED TO KNOW ABOUT MARK:

- Mark is sixteen.
- He is described as 'dopey-eyed'.
- He comes from Herne Hill in south London.
- He goes to an independent school, on a sports scholarship – his family are not 'posh'.
- He lives with his mum, younger brother Aaron and older sister Shannon. Shannon is suffering from anorexia.
- Last summer his dad died while running the London Marathon.
- The family are grieving and life at home is not easy.
- As a way of distracting himself, Mark is constantly on social media, playing games, watching porn and is constantly checking his phone. Sometimes he doesn't get to bed until 3 a.m.
- Mark lacks confidence but tries to appear 'in control' by engaging in this kind of activity. However, underneath he is a kind little boy who is missing his dad.
- Read the whole play to see what happens when Mark's obsession with sex and the internet gets out of control.

FIVE THINGS TO HELP YOU PERFORM THE MONOLOGUE:

- The internet is Mark's escape from the tedium of family life. Start by imagining the contrast between the downstairs of the house (and the stress of the family supper), and the upstairs of the house (where his bedroom is, and where he feels free).
- Since the death of his father, Mark says that he has got spotty and flabby. He has low self-esteem. See if you can connect to this feeling to gain further insight into why Mark needs this release.

- The speech is highly descriptive. Although some of the stuff Mark talks about is far from poetic, the way he describes it has a kind of lyricism about it. For example: 'Websites explode like stars on my screen with adverts and add-ons and poker sites and YouTube videos'. Think about the amount of sibilance ('s' sounds) there are in that sentence. It's like a kind of poetry.
- See if you can imagine what Mark's room looks like and what sort of device he is on. Do you have a friend like Rob who you connect with? Imagine what Rob looks like. You probably have favourite websites of your own. As Mark takes us through all the things he likes to look at, connect to that feeling that all this 'amazing' information is at your fingertips.
- When you read the whole play, you'll learn more about how Mark is coping with the sudden death of his father. At the root of the monologue is Mark's grief. The internet is like a soft blanket that protects and distracts him from feeling sad. You don't need to actively show us that Mark is sad – in fact, he is happy here – but remember it is there. Perhaps you too have a favourite thing that you like to do when you are feeling down.

Mark

" I get home and play *FIFA*, *COD*, and let Aaron hit me in the head with the sofa cushions till Mum comes home from work. We eat pizza, Shannon won't have the cheese or the crusts, Mum sighs. I go upstairs and log on, I log on for seven hours.

And it's like my whole room opens up, space, time and all the continuums. My desk is just a small spaceship that floats around, spinning, orbiting this – I dunno massive gateway of stuff – all the stuff in the world and it is amazing, because I can get Google to speak to me in French and I can play cock or balls on Skype with Rob till 3 a.m., play World of Warcraft with some dicks from Salisbury, watch a load of porn in a range of languages and get asked out by three paedos in Malta.

Websites explode like stars on my screen with adverts and add-ons and poker sites and YouTube videos. I sign up for web forums, DJ sites, I enter competitions to win Virgin Mobile goodies, tickets to V Festival and a chance to meet Taylor Swift. I watch a documentary on extra-terrestrial beings and learn what an infected cock ring looks like. I am wired, awake, my mind full, my eyes fuller. I can't even blink any more but I can't stop looking, staring into this space where everyone else is. ”